THE COMING COLLAPSE
OF THE DOLLAR
AND HOW TO PROFIT FROM IT

THE COMING COLLAPSE
OF THE DOLLAR
AND HOW TO PROFIT FROM IT

*Make a Fortune by Investing in Gold
and Other Hard Assets*

James Turk and John Rubino

CURRENCY

DOUBLEDAY

New York London Toronto Sydney Auckland

A CURRENCY BOOK
PUBLISHED BY DOUBLEDAY
a division of Random House, Inc.

CURRENCY is a trademark of Random House, Inc., and
DOUBLEDAY is a registered trademark of Random House, Inc.

Book design by Tina Thompson

Library of Congress Cataloging-in-Publication Data
Turk, James
The coming collapse of the dollar—and how to profit from it : make a
fortune by investing in gold and other hard assets / James Turk and
John Rubino.—1st US ed.
p. cm.
1. Gold. 2. Dollar, American. 3. Investments. 4. International finance.
J. Rubino, John A. II. Title.
HG293.T797 2004
332.63'28—dc22
2004052772

ISBN 0-385-51223-6
All Rights Reserved

PRINTED IN THE UNITED STATES OF AMERICA

First US Edition: December 2004

SPECIAL SALES
Currency Books are available at special discounts for bulk purchases for sales
promotions or premiums. Special editions, including personalized covers,
excerpts of existing books, and corporate imprints, can be created in large
quantities for special needs. For more information, write to Special Markets,
Currency Books, specialmarkets@randomhouse.com.

5 7 9 10 8 6 4

Paper money eventually returns to its intrinsic value—zero.

—Voltaire

CONTENTS

PREFACE

In putting this book together, we've made a few choices that require some explanation.

Because having a sense of where the dollar and gold have been is crucial to understanding where they're headed, we've covered some important points in monetary history. But doing justice to such a vast subject is not the objective of this book. So we've ended up alluding to many things without adequately explaining them (dispensing with the monetary turmoil of the French Revolution in a couple of paragraphs, for example). For this lack of depth, we apologize in advance. But to help those readers who want to learn more, we list some of the many great works in this field in Chapter 22 "Good Information," which begins on page 199.

On some current aspects of the dollar and gold, we face a conflict, since James is not just an author but also a participant. So in the relevant chapters we've dropped the literary "we" in favor of "James" in the third person.

Occasionally, in building the case for the dollar's collapse, we've encountered issues that, while not strictly necessary to the story and sometimes a bit technical, are helpful in understanding the current state of affairs. So we include a few of these topics as sidebars.

And twice, we've used less common but, we think, better ways of presenting certain kinds of information. They are:

Gold's exchange rate. Generally, when gold is mentioned in the financial media, people refer to its "price." This is incorrect, because gold is not a commodity like oil or eggs. Gold is money. An old Chinese proverb says wisdom begins by calling things by their right name. And since we don't talk about the "price" of euros or yen, but instead discuss their exchange rate, in this book we treat gold in the same way, as in "gold's exchange rate was $410 per ounce on December 31."

Ounces versus grams. In the U.S., the most familiar measurement of gold is the troy ounce. But this convention is a historical legacy of the British Empire, in which the gold standard and gold itself played central roles. As British historian Niall Ferguson puts it, "The British Empire is long dead; only flotsam and jetsam now remain." And one of these remnants, we believe, is the U.S. habit of expressing gold's weight in terms of troy ounces. These days most of the world, including the U.K., is on the metric system, in which gold's weight is expressed using the gram, which is about $\frac{1}{31}$ of a troy ounce (31.1034 grams per troy ounce, to be precise). So while we stick with ounces to avoid confusion, we also give the equivalent measurement in "goldgrams," as in "$400/oz. ($12.86/gg)."

INTRODUCTION

This book, as the title implies, envisions dramatic changes in both the global financial system and the lives of ordinary people. Because what we're covering isn't what you hear on the evening news and read in the daily paper—at least as of this writing in early 2004—we expect to be asked (over and over again) a very natural, very rational question: "Why, if this gloom-and-doom stuff is as obvious as you make it sound, don't all the Harvard economists and presidential advisors get it?"

So we're providing two answers right up front: First, as a group, political and intellectual leaders hardly ever recognize major turning points until after the fact. Eminent Yale professor Irving Fisher spoke for most of his peers when he proclaimed in 1929—just before the crash—that stocks were at a permanently high plateau. After President Nixon took the U.S. off the gold standard in 1971, most Washington policy makers expected gold to plunge; instead it soared from $35 an ounce ($1.12/gg) to $850 ($27.33/gg) by the end of the decade. *BusinessWeek* magazine was firmly in the mainstream with its 1979 "Death of Equities" cover story—which ran not long before the start of one of history's greatest bull markets. Most economists and politicians failed to predict the dollar crisis of the 1970s, the junk bond implosion in the late 1980s, and the dot-com crash of the late 1990s, as obvious as all seem in retrospect.

Our leaders and opinion makers, in short, shouldn't be expected to "get it," because they almost never do.

The second answer (vastly more important, because it explains *why* the mainstream doesn't see the financial crisis coming) is that conventional economic and financial thought is operating under some dangerous misconceptions. Among them:

Debt doesn't matter. At every level of American society, from Federal Reserve governors to Wall Street economists to average homeowners, the idea has taken hold that because we've been borrowing ever-larger amounts of money for decades and we're still standing, debt not only isn't a problem, it's actually a good thing. A $500 billion federal deficit staves off recession. Homeowners consuming their home equity boost consumer spending. A trade deficit that floods the world with dollars keeps European and Asian economies moving, and in any event America's trading partners love having all those dollars with which to buy U.S. stocks and bonds.

Governments can be trusted to manage a country's currency. It's fine for the supply—and therefore the value—of dollars, yen, and euros to depend on the goodwill and competence of politicians and their appointed officials. When problems come up, the world's central banks—with a little help from free-floating exchange rates—make the proper adjustments. By and large, they're doing a great job with a difficult task.

The U.S. economy operates independently of the foreign exchange markets. America is so efficient, and dominates the world in so many ways, that both Wall Street and Main Street can thrive when the dollar is falling versus gold and the other major currencies.

Speaking of gold, it's an anachronism with no constructive role in a modern economy. In fact, because it tends to go up when national currencies are weak, it's actually an annoyance, distracting governments from their important job of fostering growth and full employment. Gold is therefore best thought of as jewelry and nothing more.

Don't worry if the above seems completely reasonable, because, as we said, these are the core beliefs of most Washington policy makers and Wall Street money managers, and their thinking determines what the rest of us are told. Economic growth, job creation, and stock prices thus dominate the evening news, while the borrowing it takes to generate today's growth ($6 for every dollar of new wealth we create) is ignored, as is the amount of debt that we as a society now carry (more than $500,000 per family of four). Also commonly overlooked is the fact that foreign governments and investors now own enough dollars to cause massive damage to the U.S. economy if they so choose.

It wasn't always this way, of course. America's first four presidents and the other framers of the Constitution would have found today's conventional wisdom to be completely unacceptable. After witnessing the collapse of many state-issued paper currencies and struggling with the debt amassed during the Revolutionary War, they designed their newly formed union to prevent it from evolving into what the U.S. has become—a country in which borrowing is a way of life, government power grows year by year, and property rights are steadily eroded.

To capture its true purpose, the Constitution should be read as an attempt to limit the power of government. The federal government, as originally conceived, couldn't erode its citizens' savings by making their money less valuable. Nor could it mortgage the future by borrowing excessive amounts of money or encouraging citizens to do the same through federal programs and agencies created for this purpose. The framers even, as you'll soon see, prohibited the federal government from issuing paper money.

But over time, these promises were either ignored or intentionally broken. We'll argue in coming chapters that the erosion of safeguards against "unsound" money and excessive debt are both the result of choices by former leaders and their constituents and, from a historical perspective, inevitable. Government, even when constrained by a well-designed constitution, always finds a way to grow, which requires it, in time, to destroy its citizens' currency. So the dollar's coming collapse and all the attendant turmoil isn't a random act of God or the result of accidental cultural trends and policy mistakes. On the contrary, it is a natural, though unfortunate, part of every society's life cycle.

And just in case you detect a partisan political message here, let us state for the record that this late in the game, it doesn't much matter whether George Bush and Alan Greenspan or their political opposites are calling the plays. After all, for the past four years the Republicans, ostensibly the champions of "limited government," have been in charge, and federal spending and borrowing have both soared. The debt creation/monetary inflation machine, it seems, is no longer under anyone's control.

The following chapters will walk you through the consequences that flow from all the bad paper and broken promises. Among them: a financial crisis the likes of which few living Americans can even imagine, with the dollar plunging and prices of many necessities soaring; a huge shift in wealth from financial assets like bonds and dollar cash to hard assets like oil and gold; and a fundamental reevaluation of the whole concept of money.

But we reject the "gloom-and-doom" label. This book offers a fair number of warnings, true, but its central message is one of optimism. What's coming is part of a recurring pattern of human history that's well under way. And the next stage is, in broad terms, predictable. So the real point of this book is in the second half of its title: By taking the right steps now, you can not only protect yourself, but profit from what's coming—and we'll show you how.

Part One

WHY THE DOLLAR WILL COLLAPSE

There is no subtler, no surer means of overturning the existing basis of society than to debauch the currency. The process engages all the hidden forces of economic law on the side of destruction, and does it in a manner which not one man in a million can diagnose.

—JOHN MAYNARD KEYNES,
The Economic Consequences of the Peace

ILLUSIONS OF PROSPERITY

During the final two decades of the twentieth century, the U.S. economy was the envy of the world. It created 30 million new jobs while Europe and Japan were creating virtually none. It imposed its technological and ideological will on huge sections of the global marketplace and produced new millionaires the way a Ford plant turns out pickup trucks. U.S. stock prices rose twentyfold during this period, in the process convincing most investors that it would always be so. Toward the end, even the federal government seemed well run, accumulating surpluses big enough to shift the debate from how to allocate scarce resources to how long it would take to eliminate the federal debt.

As the coin of this brave new realm, the dollar became the world's dominant currency. Foreign central banks accumulated dollars as their main reserve asset. Commodities like oil were denominated in dollars, and emerging countries like Argentina and China linked their currencies to the dollar in the hope of achieving U.S.-like stability. By 2000, there were said to be more $100 bills circulating in Russia than in the U.S.

But as the century ended, so did this extraordinary run. Tech stocks crashed, the Twin Towers fell, and Americans' sense of omnipotence went the way of their nest eggs. As this is written in early 2004, three million fewer Americans are drawing paychecks. The federal government is borrowing $450 billion each year to finance the war on terror as well as an array of new or expanded social programs. Short-term interest rates have been cut to an incredible one percent, and while growth is finally accelerating, borrowing at every level of society is rising even faster. The dollar, meanwhile, has become the world's problem currency, falling in value versus other major currencies and plunging versus gold. The whole world is watching, scratching its collective head, and wondering what has changed.

The answer, as will become clear in the next few chapters, is that everything has changed, and nothing has. The spectacular growth of the past two decades, it now turns out, was a mirage generated by the smoke and mirrors of rising debt and the willingness of the rest of the world to accept a flood of new dollars. Just how much the U.S. owes will shock you. But even more shocking is the fact that we're still at it. Like a family that has maintained its lifestyle by maxing out a series of credit cards, America is at the point where new debt goes to pay off the old rather than to create new wealth. Hence the past few years' slow growth and steady loss of jobs.

So why say that nothing has changed? Because today's problems are new only in terms of recent U.S. history. A quick scan of *world* history reveals them to be depressingly familiar. All great societies pass this way eventually, running up unsustainable debts and printing (or minting) currency in an increasingly desperate attempt to maintain the illusion of prosperity. And all, eventually, find themselves between the proverbial devil and deep blue sea: Either they simply collapse under the weight of their accumulated debt, as did the U.S. and Europe in the 1930s, or they keep running the printing presses until their currencies become worthless and their economies fall into chaos.

This time around, governments the world over have clearly chosen the second option. They're cutting interest rates, boosting spending, and encouraging the use of modern financial engineering techniques to create a tidal wave of credit. And history teaches that once in motion, this process leads to an inevitable result: Fiat (i.e., government-controlled) currencies will become ever less valuable, until most of us just give up on them altogether. These are strong words, we know. But by the time you've finished the next two chapters we think you'll agree that they are, unfortunately, quite accurate.

Now, what does a collapse in the value of the dollar mean for your finances? Many things, mostly bad but some potentially very good. First, it hurts people on a fixed income, because the value of each dollar they receive plunges. Ditto for those who are owed money, because they'll be paid back in less-valuable dollars (hence the disaster about to hit many banks). Bonds, which are basically loans to businesses or governments that promise to make fixed monthly payments and then return the principal, will be terrible investments, since they'll be repaid in always-depreciating dollars. For stocks and real estate, the picture is mixed, with a weak dollar helping in some ways and hurting in others. We'll walk you through this labyrinth in Chapter 17.

The only unambiguous winner is gold. For the first 3,000 or so years of human history, gold was, for a variety of still-valid reasons, humanity's money of choice. As recently as 1970, it was the anchor of the global financial system. And since the world's economies severed their links to the metal in 1971, it has acted as a kind of shadow currency, rising when the dollar is weak and falling when the dollar is strong. Not surprisingly, gold languished during the 1980s and '90s, drifting lower as the dollar soared, and being supplanted by the greenback as the standard against which all things financial are measured. But now those roles are about to reverse once again. In the coming decade, as the dollar suffers one of the great meltdowns in monetary history, gold will reclaim its place at the center of the global financial system, and its value, relative to most of today's national currencies, will soar. The result: Gold coins, gold-mining stocks, and gold-based digital currencies will be vastly better ways to preserve and/or grow wealth than dollar-denominated bonds, stocks, or bank accounts.

That, in a nutshell, is the story. The rest of this book will put some meat on this chapter's rhetorical bones, but as historians once said of Aristotle, all that follows is mere elaboration.

Chapter 2

FIAT CURRENCIES ARE DOOMED TO FAIL

Before we explain why the dollar is headed for trouble, let's return to Chapter 1's assertion that fiat currencies always collapse. An extravagant claim, yes, but also demonstrably true. The history of such currencies is, in fact, an unending litany of failure.

Why is this so? Put simply, governments are fundamentally incapable of maintaining the value of their currencies. Every leader, whether king, president, or prime minister, serves two powerful constituencies: taxpayers angry about what they currently pay and steadfastly opposed to paying more, and those receiving government help who support greater spending on everything from defense, to roads, to old-age pensions. Alienate either group, and the result can be an abrupt career change. So our hypothetical leader finds himself with two choices, the most obvious of which is to level with his constituents and explain that there's no such thing as a free lunch. Taxes have to be paid, but government largesse can consume only so much of a healthy economy's output, so no one person or group can have all they want. This looks simple on paper, but in the real world it makes the leader vulnerable to rivals willing to promise whatever is necessary to gain power.

Our leader doesn't like this prospect at all, and so turns to his remaining option: borrow to finance some new spending without raising taxes. Then create enough new currency to cover the resulting deficit. The anti-tax and pro-spending folks each get what they want, and no one notices (for a while at least) the slight decline in the value of each individual piece of currency caused by the rising supply. Human nature being what it is, every government eventually chooses this second course. And the result, almost without exception, is a gradual decline in the value of each national currency, which we now know as inflation.

But a little inflation, like a little heroin, is seldom the end of the story. Over time, the gap between tax revenue and the demands placed on government tends to grow, and spending, borrowing, and currency creation begin to expand at increasing rates. Inflation accelerates, and the populace comes to see the process of "debasement" for what it is: the destruction of their savings. They abandon the currency en masse, spending it or converting it to more stable forms of money as fast as possible. The currency's value plunges (another way of saying prices soar), wiping out the accumulated savings of a whole generation. Such is the eventual fate of every fiat currency.

To illustrate the process, here are a few of history's more spectacular currency crises. Note that they all follow roughly the same script, with excessive government spending leading to excessive currency creation, leading, in turn, to inflation and its inevitable consequences.

Rome: Barbarians at the mint. During its five or so centuries of dominance, Rome had ample time to perfect the art of currency debasement. Various leaders made their coins smaller, or chopped wedges or holes in them and melted these bits to make more coins. Or they replaced gold and silver with lesser metals, either outright or by mixing them during the smelting process. By the time Diocletian ascended to the throne in the third century A.D., his predecessors had already replaced the realm's silver coins with tin-plated copper. And to his credit, Diocletian made an initial stab at reform by issuing coins of more or less pure gold and silver.

Perhaps this newfound honesty would have had the intended stabiliz-ing effect, but the world chose not to cooperate. Rome at the time was a vast, sprawling empire stretching from Spain to present-day Syria, beset on all sides by fast-growing populations of rough Germanic and Asian tribes. Defending the empire was costly, and Diocletian, loath to cross his major constituencies, adopted the now-familiar "guns and butter" approach, hiring thousands of new soldiers while funding numerous public works projects. When he ran short of funds, he simply minted vast new quantities of copper coins and began, once again, debasing his gold and silver coins with copper. When the increasing supply of currency caused prices to rise, he blamed greedy merchants, and in 301 issued his Edict of Prices, which imposed the death penalty on anyone selling for more than the mandated price. Merchants understood the message all too well and instead of raising prices began closing up shop. Diocletian then upped the ante by requiring every man to pursue the occupation of his father. Failure to do so was like a soldier deserting in time of war, said the emperor, and the penalty for this was also death.

Among the many unintended consequences of Diocletian's edicts was an even more stratified society. The rich, because they understood the monetary debasement taking place and hoarded their pure gold and silver coins (which held their value), became even richer. But the poor were stuck with virtually worthless copper "pecunia" and became increasingly dependent on public assistance. This put an even bigger strain on the treasury and caused even more copper coins to be minted. In 301, when Diocletian imposed price controls, a pound of gold was worth 50,000 denarii (the empire's currency unit). By 307, a pound of gold was worth 100,000 denarii. By 324, the figure was 300,000 denarii, and by midcentury it was 2 billion. In 410, a financially debili-tated Rome fell to the Visigoths.

France: Twice in one century. France in 1715 was a classic victim of bad government. King Louis XIV's many wars had saddled his successor, Louis XV—only five when he took the throne—with a society that resembled modern-day California. Taxes were high, debt levels were onerous, and people were disgruntled. Then a Scotsman named John Law showed up with a solution.

The disinherited son of a wealthy goldsmith, the handsome and articulate Law had developed a novel theory about money—namely, that the more a government put into circulation, the greater the country's prosperity. In a preview of some of today's more destructive economic ideas, he also believed that monetary authorities could, by managing the amount of money in circulation, keep an economy growing briskly without inflation, thus generating plenty of tax revenue while keeping the citizenry fat and happy. He would achieve this nirvana not with gold or silver, the supply of which was limited and therefore hard to manipulate, but rather with a new type of currency made of paper, invented and introduced only years before by the Bank of England. Paper, because its supply could be expanded or contracted at will, was vastly superior to boring old gold and silver coins, said Law, and, managed correctly, would produce a never-ending economic boom.

The now-desperate French gave Law the chance to put theory into practice by allowing him to found a bank, Banque Royale, which could issue paper livres, the currency of the day. Initial results encouraged more experimentation, and Law parlayed his initial goodwill into government contracts to trade with Canada and China and develop France's vast Louisiana territories. He also had himself named Controller General and Superintendent General of Finance, analogous to today's U.S. Treasury Secretary and Federal Reserve Chairman, with the power to collect taxes and print money. Then he combined most of these operations into one of the world's first conglomerates, Compagnie d'Occident, popularly known as the Mississippi Company.

Now in nearly complete control of French finances, Law decreed that henceforth land and stock could be used as collateral for loans, enabling borrowers to enter his bank with a property deed or stock certificate and walk out with newly printed currency. The result was a self-reinforcing cycle, in which people borrowed against their land and stocks to buy more land and stocks, driving up prices and creating collateral for new loans (not unlike today's U.S. real estate market, about which more will be said shortly).

Mississippi Company stock—the glitziest growth stock of its day—soared from its original price of 500 livres in January 1719 to 20,000 livres by year-end 1720. Law's early investors made fortunes, and ordinary Frenchmen began quitting their jobs to become that era's version of day traders. As Charles Mackay recounts in his 1841 classic *Extraordinary Popular Delusions and the Madness of Crowds,* the action was so frenetic on Paris's curbside stock exchange that a hunchbacked man made a nice living renting out his broad back as a mobile writing table for frenzied stock traders. Law became an international celebrity and, on paper, one of the world's richest men.

But within the year, the paper livres cascading from Law's printing presses caused the price of virtually everything in France to soar. And in an early example of what we now know as Gresham's Law (bad money drives good money out of circulation when the government insists that they trade at the same value), French consumers began hoarding gold and silver coins and spending paper the minute they received it. By January 1720, prices in paper livre terms were rising at a monthly rate of 23 percent.

That same month, two royal princes decided to cash in their Mississippi Company shares, and others began to follow suit, sending the price down sharply. Law responded by printing even more paper money, while using his official powers to prohibit ownership of more than 500 livres in gold or silver. This thoroughly spooked the markets, sending Mississippi Company stock—and the value of the paper livre—through the floor. By the end of 1721, the stock was back to its original price of 500 livres, the French economy was in a shambles, and Law was history. Stripped of wealth and power, he fled to Italy, where he died penniless in 1729.

The lost fortunes and ruined lives of Law's experiment with fiat currency scarred the French psyche for decades. But it didn't fix the country's underlying economic malady, which was a particularly nasty remnant of feudalism. France at that time was an absolute monarchy, in which the nobility and church leadership owned most of the wealth yet paid no taxes. As a result, the full burden of a series of weak, spendthrift kings (all named Louis for some reason) fell on the ever-oppressed peasants and the growing but still-disgruntled merchant class, or bourgeoisie. After losing ruinously expensive wars with Britain and Prussia, France in the 1780s was, to put it mildly, open to new ideas.

Without dwelling on the gory details, regime change did occur in 1792, and the new government, calling itself States General, attempted to finance the transition from feudalism to democracy by confiscating church lands (nearly 10 percent of the whole country) and using them as collateral for the issuance of interest-bearing notes, called assignats. The issuance began cautiously enough, with notes worth 400 million livres. But then came 800 million livres' worth of notes the following year, then another 600 million and another 300 million.

Because assignats paid interest and principal in paper livres, the result was a massive increase in the supply of fiat currency. By 1794, there were 7 billion paper livres in circulation. A year later there were 10 billion, and six months later 14 billion. Soon the total hit 40 billion, and a full-scale hyperinflation had begun. The ostensibly democratic government then tried to force people to accept its money by (are you noticing a pattern here?) imposing a twenty-year prison sentence on anyone selling its notes at a discount, and a death sentence for anyone differentiating between paper livres and gold or silver livres in setting prices. Shopkeepers closed their doors, the economy collapsed, rationing replaced commerce, and the fledgling Republic crumbled, opening the door to Napoleon's dictatorship and yet another round of devastating European wars.

Germany: From Versailles to Hitler. In the decade leading up to World War I, Germany was an industrial powerhouse. Its currency, the mark, was linked to gold and had been stable for decades, while its industrial regions supplied the rest of Europe with coal and steel, among many other things. But as the war's loser, Germany carried some unique burdens into the 1920s. Under the terms of its surrender, it was required to create a more democratic form of government, and then to pay war reparations to France and the other victors.

It managed the first, forming the Weimar Republic. But making reparations payments proved to be more challenging. It seems that the previous government had financed the war by borrowing, expecting to win a quick victory and then squeeze its victims to pay off its debts. So Germany entered the 1920s with massive wartime loans on its books. Meanwhile, the victors, meeting at the French palace of Versailles, were no more generous than the Germans would have been, demanding extraordinarily high reparations payments. In 1921, Germany paid off about one-third of the total, mostly through in-kind transfers of coal, iron, and wood. But covering the rest would involve either draconian cuts in services or massive tax increases. And rather than impose such burdens on its constituents, the Weimar government refused to pay the balance of its reparations. France and Belgium then occupied the Ruhr, Germany's industrial heartland, hobbling its economy even further.

Faced with an exaggerated version of government's perennial dilemma, the Weimar government chose an exaggerated response, turning on the printing presses and letting them run. The supply of marks surged and prices began to rise. Caught unaware, Germans at first reacted by economizing and reducing their consumption. But when they realized that prices were rising not just for some things but for everything, they began spending their marks as fast as possible. Prices doubled in the first five months of 1922 and from there went right off the chart. A loaf of bread that cost 160 marks in 1922 went for 1,500,000 a year later, and under the stress of hyperinflation, German life became a parody of a modern economy. Workers were paid hourly and rushed to spend their paper before it became worthless. Instead of wallets, shoppers took wheelbarrows and suitcases full of bills to the grocery store. Restaurant prices doubled in the time it took to finish a meal.

With economic chaos came social breakdown. In 1922, Foreign Minister Walter Rathenau was assassinated by right-wing militants, and in 1923 the fledgling Nazi Party attempted a coup. Borrowers found themselves suddenly debt-free, while savers saw their nest eggs evaporate. A pension that in 1920 might have promised a comfortable life couldn't buy its owner breakfast by 1923. And as always, the very rich suffered least because they owned real assets—like gold coins and food-producing estates—that held their value as paper currency became worthless. By the autumn of 1923, with one dollar equal to one trillion marks, Germany's nervous breakdown was complete.

Then, as quickly as it arrived, the storm passed. In September 1923, Germany's new chancellor, Gustav Stresemann, and the head of its central bank, Hjalmar Horace Greeley Schacht, replaced the old mark with the rentenmark, which was backed with gold on loan from America to help Germany rebuild its economy. Nine zeros were struck from the currency, making one rentenmark equal to one billion old marks. In 1924, France cut Germany's reparations payments to a manageable level, and a semblance of normality returned.

But the vanished nest eggs were never restored, nor were the values of hard work and decency that had characterized prewar German society. As in France over a century earlier, monetary chaos had created a political climate ripe for a demagogue, an opportunity soon seized by Adolf Hitler.

Argentina: Do cry for the peso. Latin American governments tend to find themselves in a particularly tough spot. Thanks to the mismanagement of their European colonizers, wealth is concentrated in the hands of a few families with little interest in sharing. The rest of the population owns little and demands much from government, and politicians who stray too far from either camp are subject to capital flights, riots, and, all too frequently, coups. The result is a seemingly endless cycle of excessive spending and borrowing, devaluations, hyperinflations, and new currencies that lop zeros from their predecessors without treating the underlying disease.

But for a while there in the 1990s, Argentina looked like the Latin American country that finally got it right. After yet another bout of hyperinflation, in 1991 it linked its peso to the U.S. dollar at a rate of 1 for 1. The central bank was required to exchange the two currencies on demand and to back the circulating pesos with dollars.

And for a while it worked. The dollar link looked stable, and investors at home and abroad began to believe that the peso might hold its value. Capital poured into Argentina from all over the world, and the economy boomed. But instead of using the resulting surge in tax revenues to pay down debt and lower the cost of government programs, Buenos Aires went on a spending spree, hiring new public-sector workers and financing projects of high cost but dubious value. When even these boom-time tax revenues weren't enough, the government raised existing tax rates and levied new ones, including a "presumptive income tax" on corporate assets that hit even unprofitable companies. On the rare occasions when the leadership did try to pare back its spending, it was met with violent street demonstrations and general strikes, and quickly gave in.

By 1998, the gap between the real value of the dollar and peso had grown so wide that Argentines staged a run on the central bank by converting their pesos to dollars en masse. The boom came to a screeching halt, and newly elected leaders froze dollar bank accounts, limiting withdrawals to $250 per depositor per week. Finally, even these withdrawals were forbidden, and dollar bank deposits estimated to exceed $20 billion were, in effect, confiscated. By the end of 2003 the peso, worth $1 in 2001, was worth about thirty cents.

IS THE DOLLAR REALLY HEADED FOR SOMETHING LIKE THIS?

It's easy to dismiss history's failed currencies as interesting but irrelevant to today's world. We're vastly more sophisticated than those guys, and there's no way we'll allow the dollar to suffer the fate of the Argentine peso, and certainly not of the German mark, right? Sorry, but as you'll see in the next few chapters, the U.S. faces the same pressures as other countries and is making similar mistakes, though in many cases on a much bigger scale. With that in mind, on to the terrifying present.

Chapter 3

WE OWE
HOW MUCH???

One of the many notable things about the currency meltdowns discussed in Chapter 2 (plus the dozens of others that have occurred over the centuries) is their similarity. Whether ancient or modern, monarchy or republic, coin or paper, each nation descends pretty much the same slippery slope, expanding government to address perceived needs, accumulating too much debt, and then repudiating its obligations by destroying its currency. This repeating pattern gives us a framework for judging the present: If the U.S. is indeed headed for similarly scary times, then (1) government should be ballooning in size and scope, (2) we should be borrowing ever-larger amounts of money, and (3) we should be financing this debt by creating a mountain of new fiat currency (or its modern electronic equivalent). Is it and are we? Yes, yes, and yes, on an unprecedented scale.

GOVERNMENT JUST KEEPS GROWING

The framers of the Constitution didn't pretend to know the future. But they believed that the system best able to adapt and thrive in a changing world would consist of free, property-holding citizens and a government limited to a handful of crucial functions like national defense, ensuring fair play between the states, and protecting private property and other rights by preserving the rule of law. And for about seventy years we kept pretty much to the plan. But as the founders and their ideas drifted further into the past, government began to extend its reach and redefine its powers. The Civil War, in particular, turned the relationship of federal government and states on its head by concentrating control over banking and money in Washington. Still, by the end of the nineteenth century the U.S. was, to modern eyes, a model of small government and sound money.

Then came the twentieth century, with its endless parade of pressing needs. World War I had to be paid for, of course. And the widespread misery of the Great Depression spawned "New Deal" welfare programs like Social Security, public works projects like the Tennessee Valley Authority, and a centralized bank regulatory regime. From 1930 to 1940, federal spending as a share of gross domestic product (GDP) doubled from 4 to 8 percent.

World War II was both expensive and unavoidable, as was the Cold War, which institutionalized the military-industrial complex. The increasingly visible poverty—and hubris—of the 1960s produced "Great Society" programs like Medicare, Medicaid, and food stamps. And once in place, these programs took on a life of their own. In 1950, welfare spending comprised roughly 12 percent of the federal budget. Today it consumes almost 40 percent. Medicare, by 1990, was about ten times more expensive than originally forecast.

From almost any perspective, the arc of government's growth is shockingly steep. In 1800, Washington spent only $20 per U.S. citizen; in 2003, it spent $7,800. In the 1920s, the federal government took only 5 percent of national income; today it takes nearly 25 percent. Meanwhile, state and local government spending has risen twice as fast as GDP since World War II and now gobbles up about $5,000 per citizen each year. In 1946, there were 2.3 state and local government employees for every 100 citizens. Today there are 6.5. By the end of 2003, federal, state, and local governments employed 21.5 million peo-

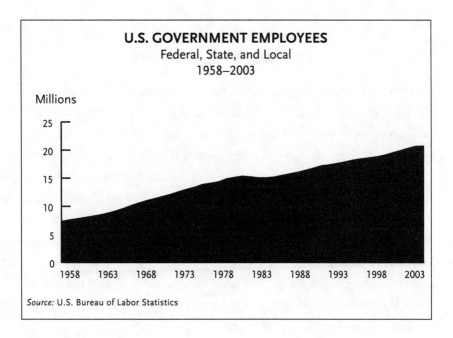

U.S. GOVERNMENT EMPLOYEES
Federal, State, and Local
1958–2003

Millions

Source: U.S. Bureau of Labor Statistics

ple, up from 8.5 million in 1960 and 4.5 million in 1940. More Americans now work in government than in manufacturing.

Government regulations, which impose (sometimes considerable) costs on business, thus slowing economic growth, have more than kept pace with spending. The *Federal Register,* Washington's regulatory bible, contained 4,000 pages when it was created in 1936. By 1950 it had grown to 12,000 pages, by 1980 to 40,000 pages, and today it runs upward of 70,000.

Add it all up, and in 2003 "the cost of federal, state, and local government in America has exceeded the $3 trillion mark," writes Stephen Moore, Institute for Policy Innovation Research Fellow and President of the Club for Growth. "Not only does the United States spend more than the entire economy of France, but government spends more money in just a single year than it spent combined from 1781 to 1900—even after adjusting for inflation."

DEBT LEVELS ARE SOARING

At each step in this process of government expansion, U.S. presidents and legislators have faced the classic menu of choices: restrain spending, raise taxes, or borrow and debase the currency. And at each stage they, like most of their predecessors throughout history, have opted for the quick fix, spending whatever is necessary to satisfy their constituents and borrowing to keep tax hikes to a minimum. The result has been a steady increase in what the government owes, and a steady decrease in what a dollar will buy. Even in the 1990s, when a few years of surpluses led most of us to believe that the debt monster had been slain, the federal government took on $2.8 trillion of new debt, and by the end of 2003, Washington owed nearly $7 trillion. That's about $22,000 per citizen, or $88,000 per family of four.

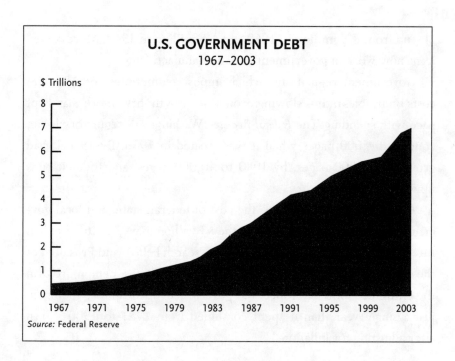

U.S. GOVERNMENT DEBT
1967–2003

$ Trillions

Source: Federal Reserve

Where do we go from here? Straight up, by the looks of it. With the war on terror as its latest rationale, Washington has turned on the spigot full blast. The federal budget, including some huge increases in nonmilitary spending, exceeded $2.2 trillion in 2003—and new federal borrowing exceeded $500 billion. That's another $5,600 piled on our hypothetical family of four.

And Washington's actual borrowing, huge though it is, may not be the worst news. The government debt chart on the previous page does not include the "unfunded liabilities" of Social Security and Medicare. This is the present value of what these programs will have to pay out under current benefit promises, minus what they've collected so far. Until recently, the number was thought to be in the $4 trillion range, big to be sure, and very real, since cutting benefits to senior citizens, almost impossible today, will become even harder as baby boomers begin to retire.

But in early 2003, the Treasury Department reran the numbers according to the tougher standards that apply to the private sector and discovered that those unfunded liabilities weren't $4 trillion, but *$43 trillion.* This revelation didn't appear in the government's official budget. But neither did the Treasury refute its economists' calculations. Why is the number so huge? Because, put simply, we're getting very old very fast. Right now, there are about four workers supporting every Social Security and Medicare recipient. But as birthrates fall and populations age (as they're doing all over the industrialized world), a few decades down the line there will be only two workers to support each U.S. retiree. Meanwhile, the cost of medical care is soaring, implying that each retiree will demand vast sums from open-ended programs like Medicare. Put the two trends together and you get massive costs in later years, which we aren't funding adequately. So if you think the pressure on the U.S. government to expand is intense today, you haven't seen anything yet.

But wait, there's more. It turns out that government, this time around, isn't the only offender. The rest of American society has now joined in the debt binge:

Households. Our spending patterns tend to reflect our collective mood. So the 1990s, predictably, saw a surge in demand for SUVs, plastic surgery, and high-end homes, among many other indulgences of the upwardly mobile. When times are tough, on the other hand, we typically scale back a little, putting off that nice vacation, keeping the old car running for an extra year or two, and paying off some debt. Banks usually respond the same way, tightening their lending criteria and cutting off their less-creditworthy customers. The result is a small decline in the amount of debt carried by individual Americans, or at least a slowdown in its growth.

In light of the tech-stock crash, the mini-recession of 2001, and the World Trade Center attacks, you might expect American consumers to have spent the early years of this decade in full financial retreat, borrowing less and building up cash in anticipation of more bad news. Instead, between 2000 and 2003, consumers put the pedal to the metal financially speaking, borrowing more than ever before. And lenders, instead of pulling back, supplied credit to all comers: Bad credit, no credit, no problem!

If you have a mailbox, you know what the credit-card companies are up to. In the past few years, card issuers like Providian and Capital One have made fortunes by blanketing the world with "preapproved" plastic. U.S. automakers are taking the same approach, via the zero-down, zero-percent loans that General Motors and Ford embraced with such gusto in 2002 and 2003.

And then there's the mortgage boom. In 2000, Americans noticed that unlike tech stocks, home values were still rising, so they began cashing out their remaining shares to buy ever-larger homes. And they discovered that thanks to innovations like home-equity credit lines and cash-out refinancings (where a homeowner refinances for more than their old mortgage and pockets the difference), they could use their homes as piggy banks, drawing down their home equity and spending it to maintain their lifestyles. From 1988 to 1997, mortgage borrowing averaged about $220 billion annually, but in 2002 and 2003 the average soared to more than $700 billion. Since 1995, the amount of mortgage

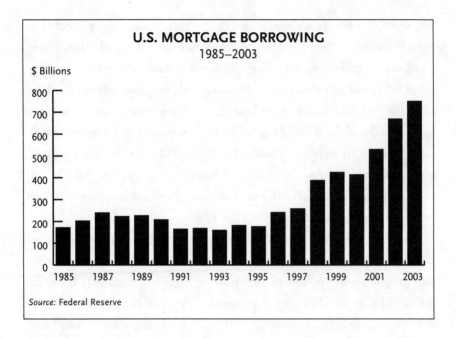

U.S. MORTGAGE BORROWING
1985–2003

$ Billions

Source: Federal Reserve

debt outstanding has doubled, to nearly $7 trillion. And everyone is piling on. Mortgage specialists like Countrywide Credit boomed in the first few years of the decade, and commercial banks like Wells Fargo and Bank One handed out home-equity credit lines the way they once gave away toasters.

Why, exactly, are all these bright bankers and credit analysts willing to lend more money than ever before to increasingly strapped consumers? For one thing, their executives are so desperate to boost their stock options by pleasing Wall Street that they're blind to the consequences (or they see the consequences but hope to have long since ridden off into the sunset with a fat retirement package). But there's another reason, a little more technical but vastly more important: Thanks to something called securitization, it's no longer the banks' (or credit-card or auto companies') money.

To understand the role securitization plays in the current blow-off stage of the U.S. debt buildup, consider how lending used to work. In, say, 1980, if a bank gave you a mortgage or car loan, they expected to keep that loan on their books until you paid it off. They had little choice. Consumer loans were all different; some would be paid off quickly, some later, and some not at all. Because analyzing and valuing this kind of credit grab bag was so complicated, outside investors had no interest in buying this debt at anything other than fire-sale prices, so the originators of the loans were stuck with them. This tied up their capital, making them look and feel like Old Economy companies, which they were, for the most part. But it also gave them an incentive to lend wisely, since they had to live with the results.

Then, in the mid-1980s, Wall Street's financial engineers had a seminal insight—that a bunch of small, dissimilar loans could be bundled together, dressed up, and turned into high-grade bonds that investors the world over would covet. And now hundreds of billions of dollars of mortgages, car loans, and credit-card debt are being packaged and sold to an insatiable global bond market each year. Lenders, as a result, have lost their inhibitions, since whatever mistakes they make in judging a borrower's ability to pay off the loan will hurt only the people who buy

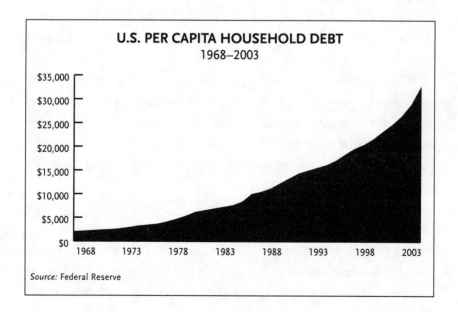

U.S. PER CAPITA HOUSEHOLD DEBT
1968–2003

Source: Federal Reserve

the bonds, and not for a few years in any event. In the meantime, the lender makes money, its stock goes up, and its executives get nice fat bonuses. And the debt of U.S. households soars.

Business. As interest rates have trended down in recent years, businesses have been issuing bonds and commercial paper as fast as their investment bankers can draw up the paperwork. Between 1995 and 2001, nonfinancial U.S. companies took on a total of about $3.5 trillion in new liabilities. And since then, companies, like consumers, have stepped up the pace, adding another $2 trillion.

But the scariest part of the corporate debt explosion doesn't involve debt per se. It involves derivatives, those mysterious contracts that pundits discuss in ominous tones without really explaining what they are. We aren't going to explain them either in any detail, because that would take a book in its own right. But suffice it to say that derivatives are contracts that derive (hence the name) their value from something else. They come in literally dozens of flavors, ranging from the familiar stock option to things that only a mathematician can fully grasp. But all are designed to divide the risk associated with an underlying asset into pieces, allowing them to be sold to different people, each of whom is theoretically best able to handle it. And as with securitized debt, their use is going off the charts. In the past decade, the "notional" value (i.e., the dollar amount of the underlying financial instruments) of U.S. derivatives exposure has risen from an already pretty big $10 trillion to around $100 trillion. Worldwide, the figure is somewhere north of $210 trillion.

What kind of risk does this present? The complexity of these contracts makes it hard to say, other than that it does present risks, and given the numbers involved, they must be huge. As legendary investor Warren Buffett (a man not normally given to hyperbole) put it recently, derivatives are "weapons of financial mass destruction" that pose a "mega-catastrophic risk."

Total debt. Add it all up and the picture is as grim as it is inescapable. America's debt isn't just rising, it's soaring. In the chart on page 27, the

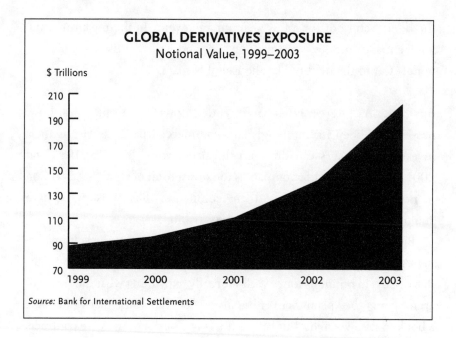

GLOBAL DERIVATIVES EXPOSURE
Notional Value, 1999–2003

Source: Bank for International Settlements

lower line depicts the growth in GDP. This is our total national income, or (at the risk of oversimplifying) what you get when you add up all the paychecks and sales receipts we generate for a given year. The other line is the total debt that U.S. government, households, and businesses have accumulated. Note that the two lines track fairly closely from the 1950s through the 1970s, implying that our borrowing was producing a commensurate increase in wealth. But in the 1980s, the lines diverge, with GDP continuing to grow at its same steady pace, and debt growth accelerating. In that decade, our debt increased by $9.5 trillion while GDP grew by $2.4 trillion, meaning that we borrowed more than three dollars for every dollar of new income we generated. In the 1990s the gap widened further, with debt increasing by $15 trillion and GDP rising only $3 trillion, a 5-to-1 ratio of new debt to new income.

As a society, we now owe about $37 trillion. That's more than three times GDP (up from about twice GDP in the early 1980s) and comes to $128,000 per citizen, or a mind-boggling $500,000 per family of

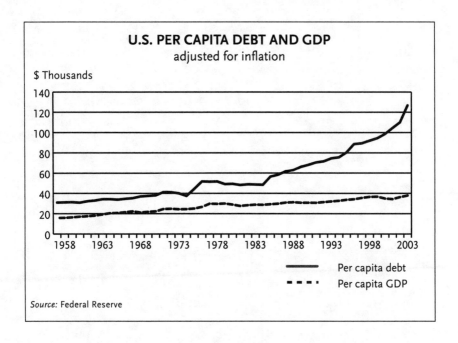

U.S. PER CAPITA DEBT AND GDP
adjusted for inflation

$ Thousands

Source: Federal Reserve

four. And the pace, believe it or not, is accelerating. In 2002 and 2003, despite a slowing economy that common sense says should cause Americans to scale back, we took on $6 of new debt for each new dollar of GDP. And recall that this calculation excludes the two biggest numbers of all: Washington's $40 trillion in unfunded trust-fund liabilities, and U.S. corporations' $100 trillion in derivatives exposure. In short, the U.S. has clearly met the first two requirements of a currency crisis: Government spending and debt are both growing like crazy.

Chapter 4

UNBALANCED TRADE

If the dollar is still a functioning currency after America's two-decade-long borrowing binge, what's to stop it from functioning forever? Well, for one thing, we're not alone in the world. Foreign investors have a say in the value of the dollar, and in the next few years they're going to say some very unfortunate things.

As a major trading nation, the U.S. exports computers, software, movies, and food, among many other things. And we import just about everything you can imagine. When we buy more than we sell, we make up the difference—known as the trade deficit—by shipping dollars overseas. And in recent years we've been buying a lot more than we've been selling. After averaging a manageable $80 billion annually during the 1980s, the trade deficit soared into the $300 billion range in the 1990s. And by 2003 this figure had exploded to over $500 billion. That's about 5 percent of GDP, a level that, when it has occurred in other countries in the past, has preceded a sharp decline in the value of the local currency.

Why are we buying so much more than we're selling? One reason is that it's a lot cheaper to make most basic products in places like China, where smart, highly motivated people will work for about a tenth the prevailing U.S. wage. So U.S. companies, in order to take advantage of this differential, are closing factories here and setting up new ones over there. Powerhouse discount-store chain Wal-Mart especially is driving the process by buying from a growing network of Chinese plants, passing some of the savings along to customers, and either driving its competitors out of business or forcing them to buy from cheap foreign sources as well. As a result, low-wage foreign factories are now flooding the U.S. with incredibly cheap stuff, much of which used to be made here. And where not so long ago our trade with China was more or less in balance, we now run a deficit that exceeds $100 billion annually.

But the imbalance goes beyond just China. We're running annual deficits with Japan and the European Union of more than $100 billion and $50 billion, respectively. And of course oil imports, mostly from the Middle East, seem headed nowhere but up. The inescapable conclusion is that U.S. consumers are addicted to a lifestyle that includes new cars, big houses, and slick electronic toys. And, as you know from the

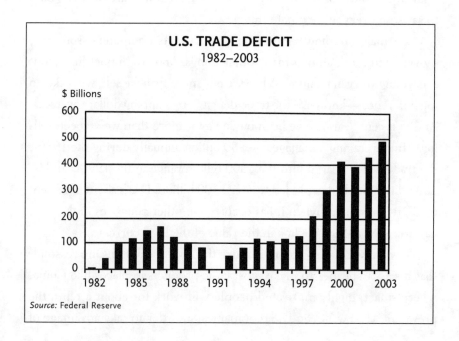

U.S. TRADE DEFICIT
1982–2003

$ Billions

Source: Federal Reserve

previous chapter, we're willing to borrow whatever it takes to avoid cutting back.

Looked at from virtually any angle, the U.S. trade situation is unprecedented. The annual trade deficit is larger than the budgets of Social Security and the military, and twice as big as Medicare. Since 1953 America's manufacturing base has declined from 30 percent of GDP (when the U.S. had a trade surplus, by the way) to about 15 percent today. Since 1985, the cumulative deficit has grown to about $4 trillion, or about $13,000 for each man, woman, and child in the U.S.

What are America's trading partners doing with these dollars? Their central banks have been accumulating huge piles of dollars as "reserves" to support their own currencies, while foreign businesses have been buying U.S. real estate, stocks, and bonds. Foreign investors now own about $8 trillion of U.S. financial assets, including 13 percent of all U.S. stocks, 24 percent of corporate bonds, 43 percent of Treasury bonds, and 14 percent of government agency debt. By the end of 2003, about a third of Fannie Mae's mortgage-backed bonds were being sold outside the U.S. In the 1980s, the U.S. was the world's biggest creditor nation, meaning that we had far more invested in other countries than those countries had invested here. But by 2003, foreign investors owned $9.4 trillion of U.S. assets, while U.S. claims on the rest of the world were only $7.2 trillion. The U.S. is now the world's biggest debtor nation.

This willingness of foreign investors to recycle their dollars back into the U.S. economy explains the dollar's stability in the 1990s. And as long as they stay willing, the supply and demand for dollars will balance, and its stability will continue. But what if foreigners change their mind and decide not to buy U.S. assets? It seems that we're about to find out. Foreign direct investment—that is, the dollar value of U.S. assets bought by foreign investors—fell from $300 billion in 2000 to $135 billion in 2001, and then to less than $100 billion in 2002 and 2003. And the dollar, suddenly, began to struggle. In 2003, it fell by about 20 percent versus the euro and yen, and by 30 percent versus gold.

But 2003 was just a warm-up. Though foreign investors recycled fewer dollars, they still bought $80 billion of U.S. assets and ended the

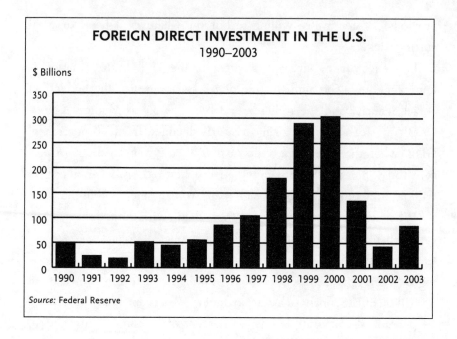

year with a bigger stake in the U.S. economy than ever before. What happens if they decide to actually start selling their Treasury bonds or Manhattan real estate? In all probability, the dollar will weaken further, causing foreign investors to look elsewhere for opportunity, causing the demand for dollars to dry up. We'll have a rout on our hands, and the debt problem will go from potential to very, very real.

Chapter 5

WE'RE ALL REFLATIONISTS NOW

Early in 2003, the U.S. found itself in what seemed, to most observers, like uncharted territory. Short-term interest rates were at historically low levels, which would normally cause both businesses and consumers to borrow like crazy, igniting a rip-roaring expansion. And though debt was indeed rising, the economy was growing slowly, if at all. The pundits, missing the point completely, were busily arguing about whether the next interest-rate reduction would do the trick.

What was going on? Simple. America's accumulated debts had become a suddenly very heavy burden. And, as all debt-ridden societies eventually do, the U.S. had arrived at a final, fateful crossroad. In one direction lay austerity, in which governments and consumers face the reality of the situation, cut back on nonessential spending, and pay off debt. This of course involves immediate pain, as the folks making SUVs and luxury homes are thrown out of work and begin defaulting on their loans, causing banks to fire their credit-card and mortgage processors and Wall Street to cut its research, trading, and brokerage staffs. The world tried this (though ineptly and more by accident than choice) after the last global debt binge in the 1920s, contracting credit and erecting trade barriers in a vain attempt to protect local industries. The result was a "deflationary" depression, in which millions of people were thrown out of work and consumers lost the will to consume, causing the prices of most things to fall.

The other road leads to "reflation," a concerted effort by the world's governments to lower interest rates and cut taxes in order to induce consumers and businesses to keep borrowing and spending. Growth, in this scenario, will bail the economy out of its mess, or at least delay the inevitable for a while.

With eighteenth-century France, the Weimar Republic, and 1990s Argentina as our guides, we could make an informed guess that most politicians will choose the reflationary path. But today we don't have to guess. The people in charge are known quantities whose past actions and public statements tell us all we need to know, and by 2003 they were in full reflationary swing. So let's begin with the chief reflationist himself, Federal Reserve Chairman Alan Greenspan.

Beginning in the mid-1990s, the global economy suffered a series of mini-crises. There was the Asian Contagion, in which the economies of South Korea, Malaysia, and Thailand imploded and their currencies collapsed. Then came the Russian debt default, the collapse of Long-Term Capital Management (a high-flying hedge fund that overdosed on derivatives), the Y2K computer bug, and finally, the bursting of the tech-stock bubble. Each was seen at the time as a threat to an already fragile global financial system, and to each the Fed reacted by cutting interest rates and flooding the system with ready cash. This added liquidity eased the markets' anxieties and convinced businesses and consumers to keep borrowing. The global economy survived, and Greenspan was hailed as a genius. Super-reporter Bob Woodward's 2001 biography of the chairman was even titled *Maestro*.

The lesson the Maestro took from all this is that financial bubbles happen, and the way to keep them from impacting the broader economy is to provide the system with plenty of cheap credit. Market forces then liquidate the bubble-related debt without unduly inconveniencing the rest of us. And since the tech-stock crash and resulting slowdown, the Fed has been liquefying with a vengeance. Between 2000 and 2003, it cut short-term interest rates a total of thirteen times, to a minuscule 1 percent. The broad money supply (the raw material that an economy turns into wealth) rose by 35 percent, and, as you know from Chapter 3, the housing market in particular boomed.

But the overall economy remained sluggish, and, true to form, Greenspan wasn't taking any chances. In July 2003, he promised to hold interest rates at their current level "for as long as it takes to achieve a return to satisfactory economic performance." He and Fed Governor Ben Bernanke also emphasized that short-term interest rates aren't the Fed's only tool. It can, if it wants, move up the yield curve, buying longer-dated Treasury notes and bonds, thus pushing down long-term interest rates and further flooding the system with newly created dollars. There's no end, in other words, to what the Fed will do to keep Americans borrowing and spending.

Over on the tax-and-spend side of the equation, President George W. Bush and his congressional allies have been, if anything, even more accommodating. Let's begin with a little background: When the government takes in more from taxes than it spends, it's called a surplus. Surpluses tend to slow the economy down, since consumers can't spend what the government takes away. Conversely, when the government runs a deficit, it spends more than it takes in and borrows the difference, which increases "aggregate demand" and pumps up the economy. Toward the end of the last expansion, the federal government ran surpluses that peaked at 2.6 percent of GDP in 2000. But then the economy slowed (which lowered tax receipts and raised welfare and unemployment program costs), a new administration took office with tax cuts at the top of its agenda, and the World Trade Center attacks created a consensus for much higher defense spending. Put them all together, and the result has been a suddenly massive federal deficit. As you read in Chapter 3, Washington borrowed about $500 billion, or nearly 5 percent of GDP, in 2003, and probably another $450 billion in 2004.

Wall Street, for its part, is terrified of a continued slowdown. If corporations can't raise prices, they can't generate higher profits. And without growing corporate earnings, who wants to own high-flying stocks? Deflation, in short, means fewer mergers, initial public offerings, and stock trades—and far more bond defaults. So it's not surprising that some major Wall Street heavies have joined the chorus calling for lower interest rates and bigger deficits. An articulate (and from our point of view rather alarming) example is Paul McCulley, managing director of the huge and influential PIMCO family of bond funds. In various updates to clients during 2003, McCulley said the following:

> The Fed is printing twenties and Congress is borrowing twenties. And this is the way it should be, given that inflation is too low and unemployment—of both tangible and labor resources—is too high. What the world needs . . . is a coalition of the willing running printing presses and fiscal deficits to support domestic demand. . . . Reflating is all about convincing the public that their cash really will be turned into trash, inducing them to spend their cash to buy things—goods, service and assets—before it loses value, in the process generating rising inflation. . . . If the dollar goes south along the way, so be it.

The rest of the world joins in. One cause of the U.S. trade deficit is that Europe and Japan are growing more slowly and buying relatively little from abroad. Why the difference in spending patterns? Because they have serious problems of their own. Beginning with Europe, when France, Germany, and their neighbors replaced their national currencies with the euro, they laid down a few ground rules in an agreement known as the Maastricht Treaty. Among them was the requirement that no Eurozone country could run a deficit exceeding 3 percent of its GDP. But the treaty didn't specify how they should achieve such fiscal prudence. It certainly didn't force member countries to cut spending or adopt rational labor laws or business regulations. So Germany and France (again, following the standard fiat currency script) kept their massive welfare states and debilitating regulatory regimes and simply hoped that a common currency would make their economies productive again.

It didn't, of course. Both economies, hamstrung by bloated governments and high taxes, have been more or less in recession since 2000.

And their budget deficits are consistently above the Eurozone limits, which puts them at the same crossroad as the U.S.: They can either cut spending and live with the consequences, or they can continue to spend too much, run ever-higher deficits, and print however much fiat currency is needed to cover the difference.

By mid-2003 it was clear that they, like the U.S., had chosen the second road. Though the 3 percent of GDP deficit limit is written into the Maastricht Treaty, French and German leaders dismissed it as a mere "symbol." And both signaled that henceforth they would pursue growth rather than austerity. As one news account put it in July 2003, "The French appear to have seized on Germany's difficulties to push for an overhaul of the pact, which they view as an obstacle to President Jacques Chirac's spending plans." The European Central Bank, meanwhile, has been following the U.S. Fed's lead, cutting interest rates to the lowest levels in decades.

Japan, the world's second-biggest economy, has been mired in a slow-motion deflation since its real-estate and stock-market bubbles burst in the early 1990s. The culprit: massive bad debts on the books of major Japanese banks that no one seems to know what to do with. If the banks write them off, they'll be left with too little capital to finance new loans, and whole sections of Japan's construction and financial sectors, currently dependent on bank credit lines, will implode. If the banks allow the loans to fester, the country will continue to stagnate. In a vain attempt to kick-start the economy, the central bank of Japan has cut short-term interest rates all the way to zero—that's right, loans cost nothing over there. And the Japanese government has tried one stimulus program after another, in the process accumulating a national debt that, as a percent of GDP, is more than that of the U.S. Now the government—whose credit quality has already been downgraded by the big debt-rating companies—is considering bailing out the country's ailing banks by buying the bad loans, packaging them into bonds (recall from Chapter 3 how the U.S. securitization machine does this), and selling them on the global markets with some kind of government guarantee. And last but not least, the new Bank of Japan governor, Toshihiko

Fukui, has suggested that he will, like the U.S. Fed, start buying longer-term Japanese bonds if necessary.

Japan also has a problem that's the mirror image of the U.S. trade deficit. Because it runs a gargantuan trade surplus with the rest of the world, it has to manage a huge influx of dollars. It could simply let supply and demand work, which would result in the yen rising in value against the dollar. But that would hurt Japan's exporters by making things priced in yen more expensive. And since exports are about the only thing that works for Japan right now, the country's leaders are reluctant to let this happen. So the central bank has been buying dollars, thus accumulating a massive dollar-reserve position. To buy dollars they have to spend yen, which means they're running their own printing presses flat out.

So here we are. The world's major economies are all living far beyond their means and are borrowing to cover the difference. And they will, it now seems certain, continue to create as much new fiat currency as it takes to delay the day of reckoning. The stage is set, in short, for a currency collapse à la Weimar Germany or 1990s Argentina, in which the world simply loses confidence in the dollar in particular and fiat currencies in general. In such a "flight from currency," the demand for dollars will dry up. We'll spend our cash the minute it comes in, sending prices through the roof (in dollar terms). We'll shun financial instruments, including bonds and many stocks, like the plague. And we'll return en masse to the only money that is impervious to government mismanagement: gold.

Part Two

MONEY THEN AND NOW

Of all the contrivances for cheating the laboring classes of mankind,
none has been more effective than that which
deludes them with paper money.

—Daniel Webster

Chapter 6

WHAT IS MONEY?

So far we've tossed around terms like "money" and "currency" with some abandon. If this left you a little unclear on their exact meaning, you're not alone; hardly anyone thinks about such things these days. So before considering gold's once and future role in the global economy, let's examine the true nature of money.

Pick up any introductory economics text, and you'll see money defined as something that performs three functions:

- A standard of value—that is, a generally agreed-upon measurement used to express the price of goods and services.
- A store of value, which holds its purchasing power over long periods of time, to allow people to save and thereby defer their spending until some future date.
- A medium of exchange, which is easily transferred from one person to another in return for goods and services.

This is an acceptable definition, as far as it goes. But a deeper understanding of money is possible when you think of it as a communications medium. Just as spoken language enables us to convey ideas, money is the mental tool each of us uses to communicate our own subjective view of value in an exchange. Say, for instance, that a seller offers something at a given price, which represents his (perhaps hopeful) view of its value. You counter with a lower price, and you meet somewhere in the middle, at a price you can each accept. Money is both the conceptual framework in which this conversation takes place and the tool that allows you to translate each other's idea of value into understandable terms. Money thus makes economic calculation, and by extension our market-based economy, possible.

Just as a given word means the same thing over years and centuries, allowing language to convey ideas from one generation to the next, money communicates the measurement of wealth. A gram of gold is an unchanging unit of account, like an inch or a meter. It conveys meaningful knowledge by how much it has purchased over time. A gram of gold has bought roughly the same amount of wheat since the Middle Ages, for instance. And as you can see from the chart below, the relationship between gold and oil in our industrialized economy has been remarkably stable.

When a unit of account is unchanging (again, think of inches or

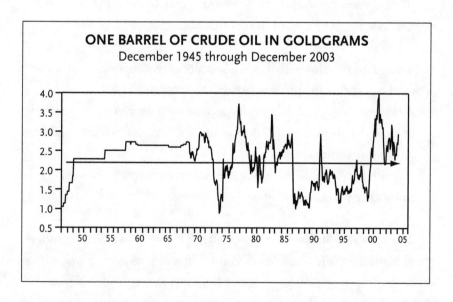

ONE BARREL OF CRUDE OIL IN GOLDGRAMS
December 1945 through December 2003

meters, which refer to the same lengths from one year to the next), the money based on it is "sound." That is, it effectively communicates wealth over time. As you'll see in the next couple of chapters, for 200 years the British pound was sound because each unit of currency was, throughout this period, defined as 0.2354 troy ounces of gold. And the U.S. dollar was sound from 1900 to 1933 when it was defined as 23.22 grains of fine gold. *These currencies were simply names for given weights of gold.*

Today's dollar, on the other hand, is emphatically not sound, because it isn't defined in any unchanging way. A dollar isn't a weight of gold, silver, or anything else. It's simply a bookkeeping entry, an IOU of the banks that are permitted by the U.S. government to create dollars. Compare the following chart to the one on the preceding page for an idea of the difference between sound and unsound money.

But sound money is not the same thing as stable purchasing power. As the gold/oil chart illustrates, over the years an ounce of gold has bought very different amounts of oil. Why? Because supply and demand for both goods and money are always in flux, causing prices to bounce around. The difference is that with sound money the fluctuations tend to

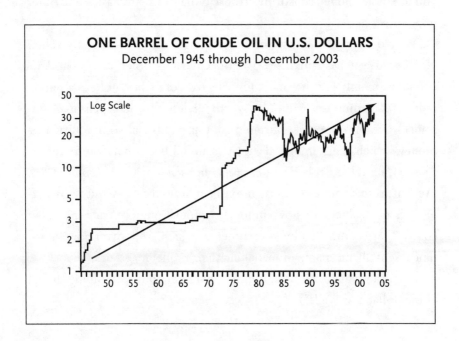

ONE BARREL OF CRUDE OIL IN U.S. DOLLARS
December 1945 through December 2003

even out over time, bringing the price back into line with historical norms. The purchasing power of unsound money, as you'll recall from Chapter 2, tends to move in only one direction: down.

Currency, meanwhile, is the physical representation of money, the item that passes from hand to hand in return for goods and services. When it takes the form of society's standard of value, as with gold and silver coins (or, as you'll learn shortly, older forms of money like goats and slaves), currency is also money. When it takes the form of, say, paper notes, currency is not money but a "money substitute." And if a currency is not defined in terms of money, but is created and controlled by a national government, it is a "fiat" currency, so called because it exists by government fiat, or decree.

In accounting terms, money is a tangible asset, while a money substitute is a liability of a bank, the assets of which may or may not be money. In practical terms, only money can extinguish an exchange for some good or service. That is, an exchange is extinguished when assets are exchanged for assets. If you accept a money substitute (for instance, dollars) when you sell a product, the exchange is not extinguished until you use those money substitutes (those dollars) to purchase some other good or service.

Why does gold—or any other successful money—hold its value? Not because it has "intrinsic" worth. Given its other uses in today's economy, mainly jewelry and a few electronics niches, gold as a purely industrial commodity would be worth far less than indispensable substances like oil or wheat. But gold isn't an industrial commodity. It is money, which is accumulated, not consumed like other commodities. As such, its value depends on *our belief in its ability to function as money*. We trust sound money because it exists in limited supply and is, by definition, not subject to government manipulation. Fiat currencies, in contrast, are controlled by governments, which are, as you now know, fundamentally incapable of managing their monetary affairs.

Keep these distinctions in mind; they're key to the unfolding drama of the dollar and gold.

Chapter 7

THE FIRST GOLDEN AGE

Over the centuries, humanity has auditioned an amazing variety of things for the role of money. The ancient Egyptians used barley; Tibetans used bricks of pressed tea leaves (pieces of which were cut off to make change); Solomon Islanders used arm rings made from the shells of giant clams. And just about every society, at some point in its development, has used livestock as a medium of exchange. Goats, camels, human slaves—you name it, we've tried it.

But virtually all early forms of money were imperfect choices, for fairly obvious reasons. Seashells are fragile, and their supply tends to surge after a good storm. Tea varies in supply with the quality of the harvest. Goats and slaves aren't interchangeable, don't hold their value over time, and, ahem, resist being divided up for change. So after much trial and error, most societies settled on pieces of metal as their money. More durable than goats and less variable than tea, metals like bronze, copper, silver, and gold could be mined, smelted, and turned into recognizable, more or less identical coins that could then be traded and stored. Bronze and copper, being more common and less attractive, became small change, while silver generally took the midrange and rare, beautiful gold became the most prized of all.

The first true gold coins appeared in Lydia, now part of present-day Turkey, around 600 B.C., and over the ensuing centuries, minting techniques were refined by the Greeks, Persians, and Romans (who, as you read in Chapter 2, designed and debased many different coins).

Once established as humanity's money of choice, gold came to be synonymous with wealth and power, and as Europe emerged from the Dark Ages and began to look outward, the search for new gold supplies became a key driver of modern history. Sixteenth-century "conquistadores" like Hernando Cortés and Francisco Pizarro led invasions of the New World in search of fabled cities of gold, destroying indigenous cultures in the process and paving the way for the colonization of the Americas. Three centuries later, in 1848, a handful of gold nuggets turned up on a Sacramento farm, igniting the California Gold Rush. Half a million people flooded the sparsely populated U.S. West in less than a decade, launching a migration that continued throughout most of the twentieth century.

THE FIRST PAPER CURRENCIES

Eventually, however, the imperfections of gold and silver money became a problem. Metal coins were too noisy and bulky to be practical in large denominations. They also wore out over time, eroding a small but significant part of an economy's wealth. So in the 1690s, the founders of the Bank of England—destined to become the world's dominant bank over the next two centuries—had an epiphany: Instead of letting gold and silver coins circulate, why not lock them in a vault and issue paper notes to be used in the coins' place? The bank began issuing paper "pounds" with the promise that they could be redeemed at any time for pound coins composed of gold or silver. Convertibility, so went this radical new theory, would make paper acceptable by eliminating questions about its true value.

The result was a conceptual breakthrough: the first widely circulated money substitute. Where money (defined as a standard and store of value) and currency (a medium of exchange) had previously been one and the same, a tangible asset, now they were separate things. Soon, much of England's money, in the form of gold and silver, sat in the Bank of England's vault, while its currency, now a liability (or IOU) of the Bank, circulated as bits of paper.

The honeymoon lasted for about three years, during which time the citizenry was happy to carry around light, quiet pound notes. But it soon became clear—in a process destined to be repeated many times in later centuries—that the monetary authorities were issuing more paper than was backed by the gold and silver in their vaults. In one of history's first bank runs, holders of pounds rushed to convert paper into metal, and the system careened toward failure. In desperation, King William III appointed his resident genius, Sir Isaac Newton, Master of the Mint in 1699. True to form, Sir Isaac got to the essence of the matter: He recognized that paper currency was an important innovation, but also that it wasn't money. Putting bureaucrats in charge of the printing presses would therefore lead to disaster.

To be viable, paper currency needed an external standard by which it could be measured and controlled. So Newton defined the pound as a precise weight of gold and linked the amount of paper money outstanding to the weight of gold in the Bank of England's vault (in the process dislodging silver, which until that time had been England's dominant form of money). Paper currency circulated as a substitute for money (i.e., gold), while gold provided the standard by which the value of paper currency was measured. Linking gold to bank-issued currency came to be known as the classical gold standard. And notwithstanding the occasional war-related interruption, it would serve the British Empire well for two centuries.

MEANWHILE, ACROSS THE POND . . .

The U.S. would eventually join the classical gold standard, but as a developing country, achieving monetary stability involved the predictable growing pains. To finance the Revolutionary War, for instance, the Continental Congress issued paper currency called Continentals, denominated in dollars and backed only by the anticipation of future tax revenues. Inevitably, wartime pressures forced the authorities to run the printing presses flat-out, and the notes soon became virtually worthless. As George Washington is said to have lamented, "A wagon-load of currency will hardly purchase a wagonload of provisions."

Returning to the tried and true, the newly independent U.S. began minting gold and silver coins in 1793, defining the dollar as $371\frac{1}{4}$ grains of pure silver. But early on, whatever coin was offered and voluntarily accepted circulated without government interference. A patron of a Boston pub might as easily have tipped the barmaid with a coin minted in Spain, England, or France as one from Philadelphia. The Spanish dollar, in fact, is described by one historian as "the unofficial national currency of the American colonies during much of the 17th and 18th centuries." To make change, it was actually cut into eight pieces, or "bits," hence the terms "pieces of eight" and "two bits."

As the memory of its first disastrous fling with government-issued fiat currency began to fade, the U.S. tiptoed back into the money-substitute game early in the nineteenth century, chartering the Bank of the United States and Second Bank of the United States to issue notes and perform some other central-bank-like functions. The banks, however, drew the ire of sound-money advocates, including Andrew Jackson, who—like Isaac Newton before him—understood the risks of using money substitutes instead of money itself. Elected president in 1828, Jackson declined to renew the Second Bank's charter, ushering in the "Free Banking Era," a quarter-century of banking and monetary practice largely unfettered by government interference. Banks began issuing paper currency against their precious-metal reserves, and by 1860, an estimated 8,000 different privately owned banks were circulating dozens of different private currencies. Most held their value fairly well within their issuing banks' territory, though the realities of travel and communication caused them to trade at discounts that grew along with the distance from the issuing bank. All things considered, it was an interesting experiment that, given the chance to evolve along with communications and transportation technologies, might have produced a very different modern economy. But like so many other promising things, free banking ended when war, this time the Civil War, was declared.

In 1861, the financially strapped Lincoln administration began issuing paper currency (which, by the way, is emphatically not one of the enumerated powers the Constitution delegates to Washington). The new currency, called the greenback, though not directly backed by the Treasury's gold, was initially accepted by northerners. But as the war depleted Washington's precious-metals stocks and massive quantities of greenbacks were printed, the notes plunged in value. President Lincoln then opted for centralization, signing the National Banking Act of 1863, which chartered a national banking system to create a single national currency. Two years later, the federal government levied a 10 percent tax on currency issued by state-chartered banks, driving non-federally chartered banks out of the currency-printing business and restricting the right of currency creation to the newly formed national banks.

In the post–Civil War years, the U.S. operated its now-centralized monetary system on a "bimetallic" standard, in which the dollar was defined as a weight of silver, and gold was measured in terms of silver. As western miners began discovering huge deposits of silver like the Comstock lode in Nevada, the supply of silver surged, and silver's purchasing power began to decline. Pressure began to mount from western states for Washington to support silver by buying up that region's growing silver production. The Sherman Silver Purchase Act of 1890 required the U.S. government to double its annual purchases of silver and turn this metal into coin. But fear that such a huge increase in the money supply would throw the relationship between gold and silver out of whack produced a financial panic in 1893, and President Grover Cleveland called a special session of Congress to repeal the act. The U.S. then adopted a monometallic system, at last joining Britain, Germany, and most other countries in the classical gold standard in 1900.

Because it represents such a departure from what came before and after—and because it was by far the most successful monetary system the human race has yet conceived—the classical gold standard bears closer examination. Under its terms, currencies were defined as a weight of gold, the way a length of cloth is measured in an unvarying unit we call the inch. Unlike today's world, where each government controls a country's internal money supply, the gold standard's adjustment mechanism was automatic and independent. Say, for instance, that British consumers ran a trade deficit with their German counterparts (that is, they bought more stuff from Germans than Germans bought from them). Under the gold standard, British gold would flow to Germany, causing Britain's money supply to shrink. The resulting reduction of credit would slow its economy and make its citizens feel less prosperous, causing them to buy less from abroad. Germans, meanwhile, would have extra money to spend and invest, thus lowering local interest rates and boosting economic growth. Some of this new wealth would be spent on foreign goods, bringing trade and capital flows back into balance.

The adjustment mechanism operated continuously, keeping individual nations from drifting too far from the straight and narrow. It didn't, however, eliminate the business cycle; on the contrary, there were some spectacular booms and busts under the gold standard. But these were mainly due to another innovation called fractional reserve banking. Because of its role in today's gathering storm, this is another concept you'll want to understand. So let's start with a look at its predecessor and polar opposite, 100 percent reserve banking.

In this system, when a resident of, say, fifteenth-century Venice deposited his savings at the local goldsmith (banks hadn't been invented yet), the goldsmith promised to keep enough gold on hand to pay his customer back on demand (though he might in the meantime use the gold to make jewelry, bars, or whatever). This kind of gold storage was more like the modern conception of a warehouse than a bank. Because the goldsmith didn't turn around and lend his customers' money to someone else, he often charged customers a small fee for keeping their savings safe.

In a 100 percent reserve system, the money supply grows at the rate of new gold and/or silver supplies, which is to say very slowly. So as technology progresses and workers become more productive, prices

would be expected to fall rather than rise each year. This kind of deflation, viewed through a sound-money lens, is normal and healthy. Such
an economy would be capable—barring war or plague—of growing
steadily for long periods of time without excessive debt accumulation
or monetary instability.

But slow and steady rarely satisfies the more excitable members of
the financial class, and by the seventeenth century, Italian and English
goldsmiths had discovered that they could lend out some customers' gold for a profit. Since only a few of their customers demanded
their gold back at any given time, the fraction of their deposits that the
goldsmiths held in reserve (hence the term "fractional reserve") was
usually sufficient to meet their obligations. And with the money they
earned by lending, they were able to pay their depositors interest rather
than charging them for storage, producing smiles all around.

Now let's fast-forward to nineteenth-century Europe, where, under
the guidance of the now-dominant Bank of England, fractional reserve
banking had begun to operate on an unprecedented scale. Say, for
instance, that a London bank received a deposit of 100 pounds and was
required to hold 10 percent of its total loans as reserves. That means it
could make 90 pounds of new loans, keeping 10 pounds in reserve. The
recipients of those loans would then deposit them in other banks, which
could then lend 81 pounds, keeping 9 pounds in reserve, and so on,
until the total amount of credit in the system vastly exceeded the original deposit. The result was a "flexible" money supply, capable of
expanding to meet the needs of a growing global economy. Of course,
flexible also means volatile. In good times, when citizens are willing to
borrow and banks willing to lend, credit grows at a faster rate than the
money supply. In hard times the credit machine is thrown into reverse,
which explains how booms and busts were still possible under the
seemingly stable gold standard.

Yet even with the destabilizing effect of fractional reserve banking,
interest rates were low in most gold-standard countries, because the
basic money supply—that is, the amount of gold—grew by only a couple percent each year. This limited the amount of paper that member

governments could print, minimizing the risk of inflation and making debt denominated in gold standard currencies attractive to investors. As a result, the four decades between 1870 and 1914 were, as you'll see in the following chapter, amazingly good times, unique in human history for their combination of economic growth and price stability.

Chapter 8

THE RISE OF
FIAT CURRENCIES

Between 1890 and 1912, virtually all the world's major trading powers joined the gold-standard club. Like the Roman Empire before it and Microsoft's Windows operating system today, gold had become "the environment," widely accepted as permanent and immutable. The result was in some ways the kind of world now envisioned by today's globalization movement: Capital flowed unfettered to its most promising uses, trade barriers were inconsequential, and economic activity was generally robust.

In this "sound money" environment, inflation was nonexistent (prices actually fell in most years) and interest rates were low, generally in the 2–3-percent range. And with the whole world, in effect, using one currency, the distinction between investing locally and abroad essentially vanished. In some years, 40 percent of British investment flowed to other lands, helping young countries like the U.S. finance the transition from agriculture to manufacturing.

Global opportunities didn't guarantee profits, of course. But free trade did offer investors the widest possible range of choices, and all in all they chose well. The result was a steady rise in global efficiency, with production taking place wherever there was a local advantage, and dramatic increases in the total amount of wealth being generated. In the six decades prior to 1914, the industrial world's economies grew at an average rate of about 3 percent annually, adjusted for the era's falling prices. Devaluations among major gold-standard countries were rare, and millions of people were lifted from poverty into the middle class.

And through it all, government's role remained, by today's standards, quite limited. This was possible because, as you'll recall from Chapter 6, the gold standard's continuous adjustments limited the ability of governments to grow, because their demands on the private sector would have caused gold to flee. This in turn would raise interest rates and slow the economy, thus offsetting the benefits of higher government spending. Put another way, under the gold standard, people were able to vote with their pocketbooks by demanding gold in return for paper. This form of instant democracy acted as a brake, at least for a while, on governmental ambitions.

When commenting on the classical gold standard, historians have a tendency to gush. Even British economist John Maynard Keynes, who later came to be viewed as an enemy of gold, referred to the era in his writings as a sort of economic paradise:

> For [the middle and upper classes] life offered, at a low cost and with the least trouble, conveniences, comforts, and amenities beyond the compass of the richest and most powerful monarchs of other ages. The inhabitant of London could order by telephone, sipping his morning tea in bed, the various products of the whole earth . . . he could at the same moment and by the same means adventure his wealth in the natural resources and new enterprises of any quarter of the world, and share, without exertion or even trouble, in their prospective fruits and advantages. . . . He could secure . . . cheap and comfortable means of transit to any country or climate without passport or other formality. . . . But, most important of all, he regarded this state of affairs as normal, certain, and permanent, except in the direction of further improvement, and any deviation from it as aberrant, scandalous, and avoidable.

Yet as it always does, pressure mounted on governments to smooth some of life's rough edges, and by the late 1800s the gold-standard countries had arrived at the inevitable crossroad. In one direction lay continued discipline, with the promise of further growth that would, over time, pull millions of people into the middle class—but at the cost of growing unrest and risk to the careers of the people in charge. The other course was that of the short-term fix, expanding the role of government to buy support in the here and now, at some undefined future cost to growth and stability.

Politicians being what they are, governments began to choose expediency over sound money. In 1883, German chancellor Otto von Bismarck created the first welfare state by instituting mandatory national health insurance, followed by social insurance (what we now call Social Security), accident insurance, and unemployment insurance. Between 1898 and 1911, New Zealand, Austria-Hungary, Norway, Sweden, Italy, the U.K., and Russia all followed suit. Washington, meanwhile, held the line on new social spending but tightened its hold on the banking sector by creating the Federal Reserve System in 1913.

Still, by 1914, the gold standard was generally accepted as the only legitimate way for the global economy to run, and the few who advocated a switch to fiat currency (i.e., currency not convertible into or defined as a precise weight of gold) were seen as fringe radicals, not unlike today's fans of a return to the gold standard. In a peaceful world, the growing desire for a social safety net might have been manageable under the classical gold standard. But before a compromise could be worked out, a Serbian gunman shot an Austrian archduke, and Europe erupted in flames. The combatants ran the printing presses, inflation surged, and one by one the major European governments severed their links to gold. By 1917, only the U.S. was still on the gold standard.

In 1925, with most of the Great War's debris cleared away, Great Britain returned to a variant of the gold standard. But, to put it bluntly, they blew it. Ignoring the fact that the supply of pound currency had surged during the war, the British returned the pound to its prewar value of 0.2354 of an ounce of gold. This created an imbalance, since there was far too much paper circulating for each ounce of gold in the Bank of England's vaults. And holders of pounds—no dummies—began converting their paper to gold. Because the paper pounds, once converted, were taken off the market, the money supply declined, causing a protracted deflation, with prices falling and debts becoming harder to pay off.

In the U.S., the extra dollars printed during the war kick-started the fractional reserve banking machine, producing a rip-roaring credit expansion. Stocks and real estate soared, as the masses discovered the joys of speculating with borrowed funds. When the inevitable crash occurred in 1929, U.S. and European policy makers responded with a series of devastating mistakes, including the Smoot-Hawley Tariff and competitive devaluations among the major trading partners. The West's economy, seemingly bulletproof just two decades before, crumbled.

Faced with massive gold outflows, Britain left the gold standard in 1931. In the U.S., savers began pulling their money out of banks and converting dollars to gold. No longer satisfied with money substitutes, they wanted money itself. U.S. banks, the gold in their vaults inadequate to meet depositors' demands, began to die by the thousands. The fractional reserve engine was thrown into reverse, as the remaining banks called in old loans and stopped making new ones. Capital-starved businesses began to fail, and newly unemployed workers stopped spending. Prices fell sharply, making loans harder to pay off and causing more businesses to close, in a downward spiral that looked, for a while, to have no end. In response, newly elected President Franklin Delano Roosevelt took the dollar off the gold standard, declared a banking "holiday," and began the confiscation of privately held gold. In light of this "continuing emergency," went his bluntly worded executive order:

> I, Franklin D. Roosevelt, President of the United States of America . . . do hereby prohibit the hoarding of gold coin, gold bullion, and gold certificates within the continental United States.
>
> All persons are hereby required to deliver on or before May 1, 1933, to a Federal Reserve bank or a branch or agency thereof or to any member bank of the Federal Reserve System all gold coin, gold

bullion, and gold certificates now owned by them or coming into their ownership on or before April 28, 1933.

Whoever willfully violates any provision of this Executive Order may be fined not more than $10,000, or imprisoned for not more than ten years or both.

Thus the government took much of our grandparents' gold, at the "official" exchange rate of $20.67 an ounce. Once the confiscation was complete, in 1934, the Treasury devalued the dollar by 69 percent by raising gold's exchange rate to $35 an ounce. We view this as theft, pure and simple, but the magnitude of the crime was lost in the cacophony of the Depression and Europe's descent into yet another disastrous war.

After World War II, with much of Europe a pile of smoldering rubble, the West took yet another stab at creating a stable monetary system. Meeting in Bretton Woods, New Hampshire, U.S. and European leaders cobbled together a pseudo–gold standard, using the U.S. dollar as the world's key reserve currency (at $35 per ounce of gold), with most other countries linking their currencies to the dollar. The next fifteen years were a brief, in retrospect understandable, pause in the march toward currency debasement. Chastened by the upheaval of the past three decades, consumers, businesses, and governments were in no mood to experiment. Banks lent only to good risks, businesses hired and expanded only when the returns were visible and compelling, workers were grateful for jobs and behaved accordingly, and governments kept their budgets in order. The result was, in many ways, the closest the world has since come to the stability of the gold-standard years.

But, alas, the 1950s were just an interlude. By the 1960s, pressures on all Western governments to expand were becoming irresistible. For the U.S., the need to contain the Soviet Union led to costly wars in Korea and Vietnam. Domestically, the growing belief that poverty could be eliminated through government action led to the creation of "Great Society" welfare programs like Medicare. As usual, the policy was not guns or butter, but guns *and* butter, financed with newly printed dollars.

Inevitably, this flood of dollars caused demand for gold to surge, and in 1968, the world's central banks acknowledged the failure of their attempts to manage their national currencies by announcing a two-tiered gold price—the "official" price and the free-market price. This just made things worse by illustrating the central banks' apparent desire to move their currencies even farther away from gold, so by 1971 the whole world was trying to convert dollars to gold. President Richard Nixon responded not by heeding the market's signal to devalue the dollar (as FDR had done) or cut government spending, but instead by ending the U.S. practice of converting dollars into gold. No longer, he declared, would the dollar be held hostage to "international speculation."

In December 1971, representatives of the major industrialized nations met in Washington, D.C., to, in effect, eliminate the last vestiges of the gold standard. In true end-of-cycle fashion, they cooked up something called the Smithsonian Agreement, which called for a deval-uation of the dollar from $35 to $38 per ounce of gold, without actually linking the value of the dollar to the metal or any other currency. Pres-ident Nixon hailed it as "the most significant monetary agreement in the history of the world."

The Smithsonian Agreement lasted all of two years, until the first oil shock and resulting global recession of 1973 forced another devaluation of the dollar, to a rather arbitrary-sounding $42.22 per ounce. Finally, with the global economy in chaos, the world's central banks threw in the towel, allowing their currencies to sink against gold, with the U.S. removing Depression-era restrictions that barred gold ownership by its citizens. The result, not surprisingly, was a wholesale flight from the dollar. Exacerbated by a second oil shock in 1978 (and Carter adminis-tration policies that made Nixon's seem economically literate), inflation soared to double-digit rates, and the dollar plunged in value versus rel-atively well-managed currencies like the Swiss franc. Gold, meanwhile, as the only incorruptible form of money, soared to over $800 ($25.72/gg) in January 1980.

Since the 1970s, the U.S. and the rest of the world have allowed their currencies to float freely, without any official link to gold. They've

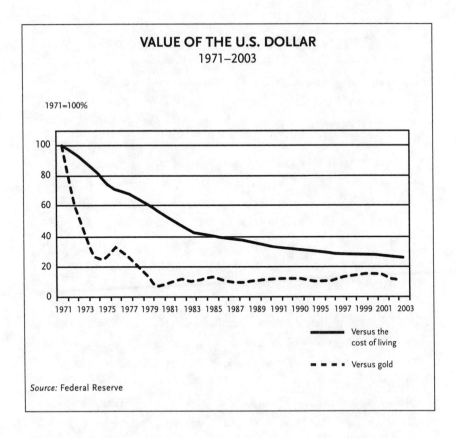

VALUE OF THE U.S. DOLLAR
1971–2003

1971=100%

Versus the
cost of living

■ ■ ■ ■ Versus gold

Source: Federal Reserve

also taxed, spent, and printed new currency at rates disciplined only by the prevailing political winds. And though inflation has seemed tame in recent years, the cumulative damage to the value of the dollar has been immense. As you can see from the chart above, since the gold standard's end in 1971, the dollar has lost an astounding 90 percent of its value versus gold, and 70 percent versus the cost of living.

INFLATION, DEBASEMENT, OR BOTH?

"Inflation" and "debasement" are terms that pop up frequently in monetary discussions and that seem, to the untrained eye, to mean pretty much the same thing. But in reality they describe two different monetary disorders.

According to *Webster's*, the general definition of debasement is "to lower in status, esteem, [or] quality." But it can also mean "to reduce the intrinsic value of [coins] by increasing the base-metal content." Debased money becomes less valuable because each unit contains less of the thing that gives it value. Inflation, on the other hand, means to increase the amount of something, in this case the amount of currency in circulation. Inflated currency loses value because of oversupply.

The U.S., following the every-possible-mistake script, is managing to both debase and inflate the dollar simultaneously. To understand how, let's begin with the concept of the monetary balance sheet, which, like a corporate or family balance sheet, is simply a toting up of all relevant assets and liabilities, in this case those of the U.S. money cartel—that is, the Federal Reserve and the commercial banks. We use the word *cartel* purposefully, because only the Federal Reserve and U.S. banks have been granted by government the lucrative privilege of creating dollars. Microsoft can't do it, nor can Chicago or New York State or any other nonbank entity.

Today's dollars are simply a liability (i.e., a promise to pay) of the monetary cartel. Within the cartel, the Federal Reserve creates cash-currency, in the form of "Federal Reserve Notes," which circulate as the paper in your wallet or purse. Commercial banks create deposit-currency, which are dollars that circulate by check and wire transfer. By aggregating the resulting IOUs, we get M3, which is the total quantity of dollars in circulation, or the total liabilities of the monetary cartel.

Now, fiat currencies are "backed" by—and derive their value from—the assets of the banking system. In the case of the dollar, these assets are made up of the gold certificates held in the Federal Reserve's vaults and the IOUs owed to the banks and the Federal Reserve. These IOUs, meanwhile, are the government bonds owned by the banks, along with the loans extended by banks to their customers.

Perhaps you see where this is going. The assets that support the dollar are gold, which is tangible and therefore not dependent on some other party keeping a promise, and the IOUs of governments, citizens, and businesses, which do depend on others keeping their promise to pay, and which therefore may or may not be worth what their face value implies. The dollar itself has no intrinsic value, since it is just a liability of the banking cartel. So the more gold backing the dollar the better, because history has proven that a tangible asset like gold is more reliable than someone's promise.

Just as a coin is debased by reducing its gold content, the dollar can also be debased by reducing its gold backing. To understand why debasement is a bad thing, recall that when gold and silver coins circulated as currency, they had two values—the weight of metal they contained and the "face value" stamped on them. Coins were normally exchanged—that is, were used as currency—at their face amount, even if the precious-metal content was less than the required weight because the coin was worn. Periodically, old coins went out of circulation and new coins were minted to replace them, with the issuer providing the silver or gold to replace the metal in the coin that was dissipated from use. But if the credit worthiness of the issuer—the government—was called into question, people stopped accepting underweight (debased) coins and exchanged their debased coins for new ones. Banks soon ran out of new coins, and a monetary crisis ensued.

Armed with this understanding, let's see what's happening to the dollar. The table on the next page contains two snapshots of the U.S. monetary balance sheet, one from 1979 and the other from 2003. As you can see, in 1979, M3—the total amount of currency in the system—was about $1.8 trillion, while monetary gold was worth about $142 billion. In other words, gold imparted 7.85 percent of the value of the dollar.

By June 2003, the picture had changed dramatically. In less than twenty-three years, M3 had grown nearly fivefold, meaning that the dollar is being inflated (i.e., its supply is surging). Meanwhile, the value of U.S. balance-sheet gold had declined by 35 percent, in part because some of it had been sold off and in part because gold's exchange rate had declined. The result of this explosion in the supply of dollars and decline in the amount of central bank gold is that by mid-2003, gold provided a minuscule 1.04 percent of the dollar's value. Like a once-pure gold coin that is now 99 percent copper, the modern dollar is a shadow of its former self.

MONETARY BALANCE SHEET OF THE U.S. DOLLAR
December 31, 1979
$ Billions

Assets	Value	Liabilities	Value
Gold @ $536.50/oz.	142.0	Federal Reserve Notes	104.8
IOUs Owed to Banks	1,666.3	Bank Deposits	1,703.5
	1,808.3	M3	1,808.3

Gold backing the dollar: 7.85%

Source: Federal Reserve

MONETARY BALANCE SHEET OF THE U.S. DOLLAR
June 30, 2003
$ Billions

Assets	Value	Liabilities	Value
Gold @ $347.70/oz.	91.0	Federal Reserve Notes	646.4
IOUs Owed to Banks	8,666.9	Bank Deposits	8,111.5
	8,757.9	M3	8,757.9

Gold backing the dollar: 1.04%

Source: Federal Reserve

GOLD AND THE CONSTITUTION

If gold competes with the dollar, is owning gold unpatriotic? Not at all. In fact, not only were gold and silver America's first forms of money, to this day they're enshrined in the Constitution. Recall that the framers had both battled an oppressive government for their freedom and suffered through the collapse of the Continental, their wartime experiment with paper currency. So they designed the Constitution expressly to keep federal power in check, in part by limiting Washington's ability to print paper money. On this subject, the Constitution says the following:

Article 1, Section 8 grants Congress the power to "coin money, regulate the value thereof, and of foreign coin . . ."

Article I, Section 10 declares that "No state shall . . . coin money; emit bills of credit; make any thing but gold and silver coin a tender in payment of debts; . . ."

The Fifth Amendment prohibits government from depriving citizens of "life, liberty, or property, without due process of law; nor shall private property be taken for public use, without just compensation."

Article I, Section 8 gives Congress the right to make any law that is "necessary and proper" for the execution of its enumerated powers.

Now, filtering these four passages through our modern worldview, the Constitution seems to present only minor barriers to fiat currency. Congress has the power to "coin" and "regulate" money, which, as long as the process doesn't involve depriving citizens of "life, liberty and property," seems to make paper money legitimate. The prohibition on states accepting anything other than gold and silver as legal tender is a roadblock, but hey, finessing such things is what lawyers are for.

So what's the problem? Well, the Constitution wasn't written with today's English usage in mind, and over the centuries, many key words have come to mean things other than what the framers intended. When the framers granted the government the power to "regulate" money, the term at the time did not mean the ability to create unlimited amounts of currency, but rather to define the rate at which two moneys—gold and silver—could be exchanged, regardless of whether the coin was minted at home or abroad. In other words, the government could mint coins—competing with the private mints that operated at the time—but not designate other things as money and create and circulate them at will. It wasn't actually empowered to "print" currency.

Meanwhile, printing increasing amounts of paper currency that becomes gradually less valuable deprives citizens of property by diminishing the value of their savings. It thus violates the Fifth Amendment. Taken together, these articles seem to make clear the meaning of Article 1, Section 10's admonition that gold and silver will be accepted as money: The framers intended the money of their new union to be "sound," which to them meant gold and silver. And they confirmed this understanding in the Mint Act of 1792, one of the first acts of the newly formed government, which defined the dollar as $371\frac{1}{4}$ grains of silver. In short, the Constitution seems to say that *only* gold and silver can be used as money.

How was paper money allowed to happen? First, the framers were succeeded by generations with no memory of British tyranny or the Continental's collapse. Government grew and, as always happens, began to chafe at the restrictions imposed by sound money, and to find ways around them. A complete explanation of the transition from sound to paper money is impossible here, but suffice it to say that it happened gradually and at each stage was opposed by those who recognized the risk. As Daniel Webster lamented way back in 1833, "We are in danger of being overwhelmed with irredeemable paper, mere paper, representing not gold nor silver; no sir, representing nothing but broken promises, bad faith, bankrupt corporations, cheated creditors and a ruined people."

The battle against paper money was legal as well as rhetorical, often reaching the Supreme Court. Yet the Court has consistently found in the government's favor—or sidestepped the Constitutional issues about the nature of money altogether. Why? Because justices don't come to the court free of political or ideological baggage. In many cases they rise to prominence through a political party and once on the court maintain sympathy, if not outright allegiance, to old friends. Courts sympathetic to expanding federal power beyond the seventeen enumerated powers granted to it were thus able to turn Article 1's "necessary and proper" language into a loophole big enough to justify virtually any action by Washington. In the case of the dollar, if a paper currency was "necessary" to government's functioning, then the court agreed that it was one of Washington's "implied" powers, and therefore permissible.

Chapter 9

GOLD'S ROLE IN TODAY'S WORLD

As the world drifted into monetary and political chaos in the late 1970s, some suggested that free enterprise and even democracy had become obsolete. The next few decades, so went the prevailing wisdom, would see a "convergence" of the U.S. and Soviet models, culminating in centrally planned economies with only limited rights for private property, all hobbled by $100-a-barrel oil.

But then, as free societies tend to do, the West found its footing.

In the late 1970s, newly appointed U.S. Federal Reserve Chairman Paul Volcker proved willing to raise interest rates to whatever level necessary to stop inflation and restore respect for the dollar. In the early 1980s, President Ronald Reagan and his ideological counterpart in Britain, Margaret Thatcher, cut taxes, unapologetically crushed public-sector unions, and confronted the Soviet Union geopolitically and economically. These gambles paid off, and the private sector regained some of its old animal spirit. Growth resumed in the U.S. and soon spread to the rest of the world, and hope began to dawn that maybe free individuals could manage their own affairs after all.

By the mid-1980s, capitalism looked more than just salvageable. It was actually winning, as stocks soared and interest rates continued to fall. With the collapse of the Soviet Union in 1990, the argument over how best to organize human society seemed to have been settled. Capitalism and democracy had won, and now the only choice was between variations on that theme. Would it be the communitarian style of Japan, the business/labor/government partnership of Germany and France, or the more laissez-faire version of the U.S. and Britain? In any event, stability and growth were now the order of the day, and in the 1990s the value of stocks and other financial assets soared, while the dollar grew stronger. Humanity, led by Silicon Valley and Wall Street, began to think we had the future licked.

While these great events were unfolding, gold, the time-tested haven from financial uncertainty, began to seem less necessary. From its 1980 peak, it began an irregular decline, finally hitting $252 ($8.10/gg) in 1999. From the centerpiece of the global money system to near oblivion in two short decades, gold's Dark Age seemed (to its friends, at least) to last forever.

Now gold plays four main roles in the world:

Central bank reserves. Though no longer formally linked to any major currency, gold is still held, along with dollars, euros, and other currencies, by central banks as a reserve asset, to support the value of their national currencies. At the end of 2002, the world's central banks held an estimated 18,000 metric tons of gold (though they claim 32,000, a discrepancy we'll explain shortly), which is about 12 percent of all the gold currently aboveground.

For central bankers, gold is both a blessing and a curse. Unlike national currencies, it's a tangible asset rather than someone's liability. And over the past few decades it has been the only reserve asset to maintain its purchasing power. But where dollars can be invested at prevailing interest rates, earning a central bank more reserves over time, gold, at best, can be loaned out for maybe 1 percent annually. Why the difference? Money substitutes exist at the whim of central bankers, who, as you now know, tend to err on the side of oversupply. So lenders of dollars or euros rationally demand high returns (known as a "risk premium") to compensate for the possibility that they'll be paid back in less-valuable currency. Gold, in contrast, can't be created out of thin air, making it relatively safe. So the market demands from it a lower interest rate.

Given central bankers' instinctive dislike of any currency they can't create and manipulate, the obvious choice would be for them to sell some of their gold and invest the proceeds in income-producing assets. And in the 1990s many of them, including Canada, the Netherlands, Belgium, Austria, Switzerland, and the U.K., did just that. At the same time, central banks were using other tools—including lending, swaps (a variant of lending), and derivatives like options—to turn their gold into cash. Lending, for instance, involves the central bank transferring gold to a major private bank, known as a bullion bank, which pays the central bank a small-but-positive interest rate, then sells the gold on the open market. By the end of 2003, about 14,000 of the central banks' 32,000 tonnes of gold had been lent in this way. But the banks were able to claim ownership of the entire 32,000 tonnes, because under their somewhat deceptive reporting rules, they're able to combine gold still sitting in their vaults and gold they've loaned out into one accounting entry.

By 1999, central-bank selling and lending (and bullion-bank selling) had pushed gold's price below $300 an ounce ($9.64/gg), causing concern about its impact on gold-producing nations and central banks that had chosen not to sell. So the major European central banks hammered out the Washington Agreement on Gold (WAG), which limited the eleven Eurozone countries, plus the European Central Bank and those of Sweden, Switzerland, and the U.K., to total sales of 400 tonnes a year through 2004. The participants also agreed not to increase their gold lending over the term of the pact. Coincidentally, 1999 saw gold's low for this cycle of $252/oz. ($8.10/gg).

Coins. Another way for central banks to "dishoard," or sell, their gold is to mint coins. Besides popular coins like the Canadian Maple Leaf and U.S. Gold Eagle, it is now possible to buy coins minted by Austria, South Africa, Australia, China, and France, among others. At 100 tonnes a year, this is a small part of the gold market in any one year, though cumulatively it has become important.

Jewelry. According to the World Gold Council, gold jewelry demand accounts for a whopping 3,000 tonnes each year. But this statistic is deceptive. In truth, as much as 80 percent of the gold jewelry produced each year is sold to Asians and Middle Easterners, who view it in the same way that Westerners view gold coins—as money.

Industrial applications. Gold, it turns out, has characteristics that make it perfect for twenty-first century high tech. It is malleable, reflective, corrosion-resistant, and an unparalleled thermal and electrical conductor. So the electronics industry finds it either useful or indispensable in computers, televisions, smart weapons, spacecraft, you name it. Gold alloys line rocket engines, gold wires connect components in printed circuit boards, and gold contacts line the keypads of touch-tone phones. The list is long and growing quickly. But at only 50 tonnes a year, industrial demand isn't yet a significant part of gold's story.

Part Three

WHY GOLD WILL SOAR

Three or four or five years from now we'll look back at today's price of $400 gold and ask ourselves, "Where the devil were we? What were we thinking about? Gold at $400 was cheaper than dirt. Why didn't we recognize this back in the year 2003?"

—RICHARD RUSSELL, editor,
Dow Theory Letters

Chapter 10

GOLD'S FUNDAMENTALS ARE POSITIVE

Between soaring U.S. debt levels and the Fed's willingness to flood the world with dollars, it's easy to make the case that gold's long-term future is as bright as it's ever been. But what about the near term? Predicting year-ahead price action for any asset class is tricky, and gold, with its sensitivity to political as well as economic currents, is trickier than most. But tricky does not mean impossible. The way a Wall Street analyst might look at stocks versus bonds and conclude that one or the other is undervalued, it's possible to use gold's supply/demand trends and value relative to other assets to gain an idea of how it should behave in the short run. Here are two such approaches, both of which (surprise) are flashing screaming buy signals:

GOLD IS CHEAP RELATIVE TO STOCKS

No asset, including gold, exists in a vacuum. Stocks, bonds, real estate, and precious metals all compete for the same limited pool of capital, which means that for gold to be attractive, its prospects must be not just good, but better than those of, say, growth stocks. One way of making this comparison is the Dow/gold ratio, which computes how much

gold it takes to buy the Dow Jones Industrial Average of major American stocks. As you can see from the chart below, this relationship has
been rather volatile.

In 1971, gold was $40 per ounce ($1.28/gg) and the Dow was 890,
meaning that it took about 22 ounces of gold to buy the Dow. Nine years
later, less than one ounce would buy the Dow. By the end of 1999, the
two had diverged once again, with gold at $279/oz. ($8.90/gg) and the
Dow at about 11,497, for a Dow/gold ratio of 41, far higher than its
early-1970s peak. But note that this time around, both numbers in the
ratio have an extra zero. That's because of inflation. A dollar purchases
today what 10 cents purchased in 1971, so we need 10 times as many
dollars to buy an ounce of gold or the Dow Industrials.

A Dow/gold ratio at the high end of its range implies two things.
First, if historical relationships hold, gold is more likely to rise versus
stocks in coming years than to fall. Second, the distance between the

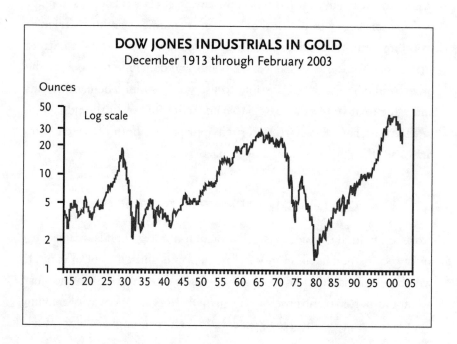

DOW JONES INDUSTRIALS IN GOLD
December 1913 through February 2003

1971 high and 1980 low gives a hint of how far gold can run this time around, especially with the financial gale now at its back.

MONETARY DEMAND IS ABOUT TO SURGE

One of the shocking things about gold is how little there is of it. In our sometimes frantic 4,000 years of searching, we've found perhaps 135,000 tonnes. Today, the world's entire hoard of gold would occupy a single (admittedly very heavy) cube 60 feet on a side—equivalent to the volume of three good-sized houses or the bottom 10 percent of the Washington Monument. To put this in perspective, the U.S. produces about 240,000 tonnes of steel *each day*.

But unlike steel, where production can be expanded by simply building more factories, the supply of gold increases only when we find and mine new deposits. Since 1492, there has never been a year in which the world's above-ground gold stock increased by more than 5 percent. The nineteenth-century average was about 2 percent, which is one reason that inflation was nonexistent for gold-standard currencies: The world's money supply was constrained by nature to a low-single-digit growth path.

Although gold no longer circulates as currency, it still has both monetary and commercial uses. The demand from these sources is estimated at around 4,000 tonnes each year. The output of the world's gold mines is currently about 2,500 tonnes, creating an annual supply shortfall of more than 1,500 tonnes, or approximately 50 million ounces.

For most commodities, a supply/demand imbalance of this size would cause either the price or the level of production, and probably both, to soar. But commodities are consumed after they're produced, and gold, remember, is not just a commodity. Gold is money, which, once discovered, tends to be hoarded. So the vast bulk of what has been mined is still around, and the current deficit is covered by owners of previously mined gold. Central banks, as you know, sell and/or lend millions of ounces per year, which, together with other forms of "dishoarding," like people selling their jewelry and gold coins, fills the gap. So while an annual supply shortfall of 50 million ounces is clearly a positive, absent a big jump in demand, aboveground stocks of gold are more than sufficient to make up the difference. In other words, *current mine production is far less important for gold's exchange rate than are trends in demand.*

And on the demand front, things are looking up, thanks to the emergence of Asia's sleeping giants. The whole world is setting up factories in China, both to exploit its cheap, highly motivated workforce and to gain access to a billion new consumers. This is bad news for U.S. and European factory workers, but for China, the result is an embarrassment of riches, including a trade surplus that exceeds $100 billion a year with the U.S. alone. By the end of 2003, China's foreign exchange reserves—mostly in the form of dollars—exceeded $400 billion. And Chinese leaders, showing an historical savvy currently lacking in the West, were eyeing gold. Beijing is rumored to be buying much of the gold Western central banks are selling (and considerably more than the annual 100 tonnes it reported to the International Monetary Fund the past two years).

In 2002, Beijing removed the Communist-era ban on its citizens owning gold. In a survey quoted in the Hong Kong edition of *China Daily,* 20 percent of Chinese respondents said they were willing to move 10 to 30 percent of their savings into gold. An analyst quoted in the same story put the resulting increase in gold demand at about $36 billion, or about 300 tonnes annually.

India, meanwhile, is attracting almost as much foreign capital as is China, and in October 2003 ended a four-decade ban on bullion trading. Because India has traditionally been a huge market for precious metals (much of the gold mined in the West already ends up in Indian safes or adorning Indian women), the combination of rising incomes and more liberal ownership rules should have the same effect there as in China.

How will this suddenly much wider gap be filled? It's possible that central banks—which, as you'll see shortly, are more concerned with minimizing gold's exchange rate than maximizing the value of their gold reserves—will step up their sales. And they'll certainly try to talk the exchange rate down through anti-gold propaganda. But neither will do the trick, because government resources—of both gold and public credulity—are limited. Much more likely is that gold's exchange rate will rise until the rest of us start converting our jewelry and coins into dollars.

Chapter 11

THE FEAR INDEX:

WE'RE JUST BEGINNING TO WORRY

Perhaps the single best gauge of where gold is headed in the next couple of years is called the Fear Index. As its name implies, it measures our anxiety about the dollar and the U.S. monetary and banking system, and in the twenty years since James invented it, each of its "buy" signals has been followed by a marked, sometimes spectacular, increase in gold's exchange rate.

To understand how the Fear Index works, recall from Chapter 8's discussion of inflation versus debasement that the dollar is a balance-sheet currency, which is to say an accounting fiction. Its value is derived from the assets held by the Federal Reserve and commercial banks, some of which, like gold, are real and tangible, and some, like bank loans, foreign currencies, and derivatives, are not. The Fear Index measures the relative importance of gold in this mix and is calculated by multiplying the U.S. gold reserve (i.e., the weight of gold reportedly under the Treasury's control) by gold's exchange rate to get its total market value, and dividing this result by M3, the broadest measure of money supply.

$$\frac{(\text{US Gold Reserve}) \times (\text{Gold's Market Price})}{M3} = \text{Fear Index}$$

A reading of, say, 2 percent, indicates that for every $100 circulating as M3, there is gold worth $2 sitting in the U.S. Treasury's vaults. Gold thus accounts for 2 percent of the dollar's value, with the other 98 percent dependent on the Fed's financial assets along with those of the nations' banks. The calculation for December 31, 2003, is as follows:

$$\frac{(261.5 \text{ million ounces of gold}) \times (\$415.00 \text{ per ounce})}{\$8,850 \text{ billion (M3)}} = 1.23 \text{ percent}$$

When the Fear Index is falling (that is, when the number of dollars in circulation is rising faster than the market value of the gold in U.S. reserves, or when the number of dollars is falling more slowly than the value of the gold reserves), the implication is that people are willing to hold these extra dollars because they're optimistic about the prospects of the dollar and/or the U.S. economy. When the Fear Index is rising (which occurs when money is flowing into gold, pushing up its exchange rate and raising the market value of U.S. gold reserves), it's usually because people are worried about the dollar or the health of the U.S. banking system and are looking for alternative stores of value.

When the Fear Index exceeds its 21-month moving average* and the moving average rises above its level of the previous month, the result is a "buy" signal, indicating that gold is headed higher. As you can see from the chart on the next page, there have been only five such signals in the past thirty-five years, all of which were followed by gold rallies. So let's look at each in turn:

MAY 1972

As you know, from 1934 to 1971, the U.S. government pegged the gold/dollar exchange rate at $35 an ounce (which is to say that it

---

* A moving average is the average price for a security or commodity for a given time frame. To calculate a 21-day moving average for gold, add up its closing exchange rates for the most recent 21 market days and divide by 21.

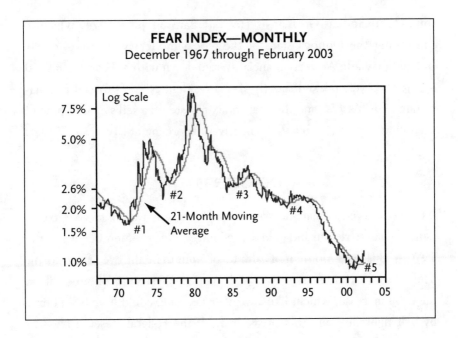

defined the dollar as ⅟₃₅ of a troy ounce) and was obligated to accept requests by other countries to redeem dollars for gold on demand. But in the 1960s, the dollar was being debased both by a credit expansion engineered by U.S. banks and the reckless "guns and butter" deficit-spending policies of the federal government. During this time, it was becoming increasingly apparent that one ounce of gold was worth more than $35. As doubts about the dollar's future escalated, dollar redemptions threatened to exceed U.S. gold reserves.

But rather than devalue the dollar as President Roosevelt had done, President Nixon closed the Federal Reserve's "gold window" in August 1971, ending dollar/gold redeemability. Anti-gold propagandists in and out of government predicted at the time that gold, without Washington's support, would wither away. Instead, it began to climb higher, hitting $59 an ounce ($1.89/gg) in May 1972 and triggering the Fear Index's first buy signal.

Doubts about the dollar were soon proved correct, as the previous decade's credit boom ended in the inevitable recession. Banks began to implode, including Germany's Herstatt Bank in June 1974, which—illustrating the tenuous state of the global monetary regime—nearly pulled the whole Western financial system down with it. Fear was indeed rising. The cycle peaked shortly after President Nixon's forced resignation in August 1974, and the Fear Index registered a sell signal in June of the following year, with gold up nearly 300 percent, at $162 ($5.21/gg).

OCTOBER 1977

As it became clear that the West, though shaken, would survive, confidence began to return and gold drifted lower. But—remember, it was the 1970s—this brief moment of calm turned out to be the eye of the storm. The oil shock had affected energy-dependent Western economies like a huge tax increase, which, like any other tax hike, could have been offset by belt-tightening in other areas. Instead, the Federal Reserve tried to minimize the short-term pain by flooding the system with money, and the banks again expanded credit excessively, with the inevitable result—the dollar was further debased. Interest rates fell and gold bounced to $161 ($5.18/gg), causing the Fear Index to flash another buy signal in October 1977. The world, right on cue, then proceeded to go briefly insane, with oil spiking again, the dollar collapsing against the Swiss franc, German mark, and other major currencies, Iranian militants seizing several hundred American diplomats, and the Soviets invading Afghanistan. Inflation soared to double-digit rates not seen in living memory. And gold, as the only stable form of money available to most Americans, rose steadily for a while and then exploded, hitting $850 ($27.33/gg) in January 1980. Gold proved to be more than an inflation hedge—it was a refuge for a monetary system gone awry—and the Fear Index peaked at 9.4 percent, nearly six times its level just nine years before.

Notwithstanding this upheaval, the system held together. Newly appointed Federal Reserve Chairman Paul Volcker began reducing the growth rate of M3 (which, you'll recall, is the denominator of the Fear Index formula), and the Index soon fell below its moving average, flashing a sell signal in January 1981, with gold at $507 ($16.30/gg).

JULY 1986

The early-Volcker/Reagan-era's combination of tight money, lower taxes, and plunging energy prices sent the Fear Index into a sustained decline. It briefly crossed above its 21-month moving average in 1982, in response to the Penn Square Bank crisis and Mexican debt default, but failed to generate a buy signal when the second criterion—the moving average exceeding the previous month's level—didn't material-ize. Gold's exchange rate then drifted lower, as it does during times of peace and prosperity, eventually bottoming out at $288 ($9.26/gg) in February 1985.

But by the mid-1980s another financial crisis was brewing, with the Ohio and Maryland "banking holidays" quickly followed by the collapse of the Texas banks' oil-dependent loan portfolios. The Index flashed a buy signal in July 1986 with gold at $357 ($11.48/gg), just in time for the crisis to go international, as the dollar plunged against the German mark and other major currencies. Then came the October 1987 stock-market crash, followed in short order by the first stage of the savings-and-loan crisis, as those once-stodgy home lenders, now burdened with bad mortgage and commercial loans and portfolios of soon-to-be-nearly-worthless junk bonds, began going belly-up at rates not seen since the Great Depression. Gold climbed to $506 ($16.27/gg), or about 40 percent above its exchange rate when the buy signal was given. But once again—notice a pattern forming?—the U.S. government responded aggressively to keep the monetary system from imploding, taking over and bailing out dozens of failed banks. A meas-ure of confidence returned, and the Fear Index slipped back below its 21-month moving average in February 1988.

APRIL 1993

By the early 1990s, the global economy in general and the U.S. in par-ticular were experiencing a gradual recovery, and the focus of instability had shifted to exchange rates. European countries linked the values of their currencies and were expanding credit at a relatively rapid pace. In the U.S., Fed Chairman Alan Greenspan was maintaining the tight-money, "disinflationary" policies of his predecessor, causing M3 to actually decline in the twelve months ending September 1992. This growing imbalance between the supply of dollars and European currencies eventually caused the European Exchange Rate Mechanism to splinter. With governments feeling the pressures of disinflation, central banks slowly but surely began cutting interest rates and expanding their money supply, attempting to prod the banks to expand credit in order to accelerate growth to politically acceptable levels. Fearing a new burst of inflation, investors pushed gold to $356 ($11.45/gg), triggering the Fear Index's fourth buy signal in April 1993. Gold then spiked to $405 ($13.02/gg), before drifting down to $383 ($12.31/gg) in November 1994, where it crossed below its 21-month moving average.

MAY 2002: THE REAL BULL MARKET BEGINS

As the boom of the 1990s gathered momentum, confidence soared and money flowed into other, more modern-seeming vehicles like tech stocks and leveraged real estate. Because such assets have relatively little (in some cases no) weight in the Fed's inflation statistics, inflation seemed to decline, and gold entered a grinding thirty-two-month bear market, finally touching a low of $252 ($8.10/gg) in July 1999. In the late-cycle euphoria over tech stocks' seemingly limitless future, gold was seldom mentioned in serious financial circles. The world's most time-tested money had, ironically, never looked so irrelevant.

But overconfidence breeds leverage, which in turn breeds instability, and in the late 1990s the global financial system got the bill for its exuberance. As you'll recall from Chapter 5, the "Asian Contagion" was followed by Russia's financial collapse, the Long-Term Capital Management debacle, and the tech-stock bloodbath. And gold began to creep higher. In May 2002, the fifth Fear Index buy signal was triggered, with gold at $326 ($10.48/gg). Here's the calculation:

$$\frac{(261.6 \text{ million ounces}) \times (\$326.00 \text{ per ounce})}{\$8,135 \text{ billion}} = 1.05 \text{ percent}$$

The reading of 1.05 percent implies that in May 2002, gold reserves supported only 1.05 percent of the dollar's value. (Note that this is also the formula for calculating the dollar's gold-backing ratio in "Inflation, Debasement, or Both?" on page 60.) That's one of the lowest readings ever, and brings us to the Fear Index's other contribution to our understanding of gold. Besides being a good trend indicator, it is also a much better measure of gold's value relative to the dollar than is gold's exchange rate, because it (the Fear Index) adjusts for the dollar's debasement.

Looking at gold's exchange rate, for instance, one might conclude that because it's ten times as high as in the early 1970s, it has already had a nice run and is now expensive. But this view is flawed, because the dollar isn't the same unit of measurement that it was in the 1970s. Today it buys about a tenth of what it did three decades ago. The Fear Index, on the other hand, does account for the rising number of dollars in circulation, giving us an accurate picture of gold's real value. And as you can see from the chart on page 79, the Index (and by implication, gold's exchange rate) is much lower today than at any other time in the past three decades, making it an even better value today than it was at each of the four previous turning points.

To sum up, the Fear Index is sending two messages: Gold is headed higher in the near future, and it's so undervalued relative to the dollar that this move could dwarf anything that has come before.

Chapter 12

THE GREAT CENTRAL-BANK SHORT SQUEEZE

The aftermath of the October 1987 stock-market crash was a chaotic time. The market had just experienced its worst one-day decline in history, the dollar was in a free fall against other major currencies, and gold, not surprisingly, had risen to $506 an ounce ($16.27/gg), its highest point in six years. But gold's rally was short-lived, as the federal government dishoarded, or sold, 525,000 ounces of its gold stockpile during the next few weeks, helping to send the metal back below $500 ($16.01/gg). This was Washington's largest intervention in the gold market since the 1970s, and the timing and size suggest it was designed to stop the gold rally. Meanwhile, the fact that the Treasury's actions were barely mentioned in official circles (the decrease in the U.S. gold stock simply appeared in the Federal Reserve's weekly balance sheet) implied a desire to keep the whole episode quiet.

As a one-time response to the stock market's crash, this intervention might have been understandable, if not defensible. But it wasn't a singular event. On the contrary, it set a pattern that, if anything, has grown more pronounced in recent years. The evidence is now clear that the U.S. Treasury and the world's other central banks are using their massive gold stockpiles to keep the metal's exchange rate artificially low.

And in the process, they've all but guaranteed their worst nightmare, a massive "short squeeze" that sends gold through the roof. We'll back these assertions up in a minute, but first let's examine what central banks are and what they do.

A central bank is a financial institution empowered by a national government to manage the nation's money supply. Early on, as with the Bank of England during the classical gold standard, this role was essentially passive. The Bank simply ensured that the rules of the gold standard were followed by offering to exchange gold for pound notes on request. This redeemability feature maintained the balance between the amount of gold in its vault and the amount of money substitutes in circulation. Gold was the unchanging measure of value, and currencies were defined as a weight of the metal. This system remained in place until 1971, when President Nixon responded to growing claims on the dwindling U.S. gold reserve by breaking the dollar's formal link to gold.

Since then, the passive maintenance role of central banks, in which currency was valued in terms of gold, has morphed into its mirror image. That is, central banks have come to define gold in terms of the dollar. Because all fiat currencies are depreciating, managing gold means, in effect, keeping a lid on its exchange rate. And since at least 1987, the evidence that the world's central banks are surreptitiously propping up their own currencies by depressing gold's exchange rate has become overwhelming. One of these undisclosed interventions took place on Friday, April 11, 1997. This is what James wrote a few days later:

> The Producer Price Index was released that morning, and it rose 0.4%, far above expectations and far above its recent trend. Also, that morning began with gold and the other precious metals trading relatively firm. When the PPI was released, two things happened. As would be expected by an increase in inflation, the gold price began to rise, and the 30-year T-Bond began to drop hard. However, these trends did not last long. It appeared that **some powerful force had entered the market**. [Emphasis added.]

As gold started to move up, someone started to whack it, and they did so relentlessly. You could clearly see the chain of events as they progressed. First, the day traders who were long gold quickly recognized the magnitude of the selling, so they joined in, selling their long positions and jumping in on the short side. This selling added additional pressure to the market, which in turn triggered stops and selling by other longs. By this time the hedge funds and the commodity pools were also jumping in on the short side, and notwithstanding its promising start, the gold market was in full retreat. It ended the day down $1.60, closing above its worst levels only because the short sellers covered at the end of the day.

What was the powerful force that stopped this gold rally in its tracks? In the ensuing five years, research by James, several friends in the Gold Anti-Trust Action Committee (GATA), and various GATA allies has made the case abundantly clear: As in 1987, it was the U.S. Treasury, acting in concert with the world's other central banks. The volume and complexity of the evidence makes it impossible to cover completely in this book. The details are available at www.gata.org and www.fgmr.com. We also highly recommend that you download "Not Free, Not Fair: The Long-Term Manipulation of the Gold Price," published in August 2004 by Sprott Asset Management (www.sprott.com), one of North America's leading investment companies.

In the meantime, here are a few of the highlights:

FOLLOWING THE CENTRAL BANKERS' FOOTPRINTS

1. *Greenspan tells us what's happening.* On July 24, 1998, testifying before the House Banking Committee, Fed Chairman Alan Greenspan said: ". . . central banks stand ready to lease [i.e., lend] gold in increasing quantities should the price rise." Not only did Mr. Greenspan describe the means by which central banks influence gold's exchange rate, he clearly stated their objective.

2. *Piling on by central banks.* In May 1999, the Bank of England

announced its intention to dishoard one-half of its gold reserve. Aside from the odd timing of selling when gold's exchange rate was already low, the fact that the BOE announced the sale in advance seemed sure to guarantee the lowest possible price for their gold, a result that would clearly not be in the best interests of the British people. Think about it: Does Warren Buffett announce in advance when he plans to sell a stock? Of course not, because it would tip off other players, causing the stock to fall. So it seems that the BOE's announcement was driven by another factor, which, in retrospect, is obvious: The BOE was trying to magnify the effect of its sales by inducing other market participants to sell as well.

3. *The ESF as the government's agent.* On April 9, 2000, GATA contributor Reg Howe published "The ESF and Gold: Past as Prologue?", which revealed some rather startling information about the Exchange Stabilization Fund, a quasigovernmental agency that reports only to the President and Treasury Secretary. Created subsequent to the 1933 gold confiscation, and funded by the paper profits arising from the 1934 devaluation of the dollar against gold, the ESF is shrouded in mystery and, as an exclusive domain of the executive branch, operates largely outside of congressional oversight. Howe noted that unexplained losses were appearing in the ESF's quarterly reports to Congress in quarters when the gold price went up, while profits were earned in quarters when the gold price fell. This result was curious, because the Treasury, both in public statements and letters in response to queries, maintained that no interventions in the foreign exchange markets were taking place. As Howe observed, "there were no other obvious activities that might explain [these] losses." His conclusion: The ESF was intervening in the gold market.

4. *The Smoking Gun.* In December 2000, James discovered that irrefutable evidence of the U.S. government's intervention in the gold market was available from its own public reports. Without going into the calculations here (they're available at www.fgmr.com, under "The Smoking Gun"), suffice it to say that the reports revealed a discrepancy of one million ounces of gold due to a transaction undertaken by the ESF. And

though this was one of the larger discrepancies, they were occurring month after month. In other words, contrary to what the U.S. government was telling the world, it was indeed intervening in the gold market.

5. *The Fed rewrites history.* After publishing these findings, James wondered how the Treasury would explain this discrepancy between the ESF's activity in the gold market and their previous statements that neither the U.S. Treasury nor the ESF was trading gold. The answer came quickly. In February 2001, the Federal Reserve began covering its tracks, not only dropping all reference to the ESF in its subsequent U.S. Reserve Assets report, but going back and *changing already published reports.* Not only were the figures changed, but all the previous references to the ESF were eliminated.

6. *The Fed slips up.* In early 2001, the Federal Reserve released the minutes of its Open Market Committee meetings in 1995. Not only were these minutes five years old, but the minutes were redacted, thus keeping parts of the proceedings secret. But in the transcript of the Fed's January 31, 1995, meeting, somebody forgot to redact some very revealing words about the ESF and its activity with gold. Here's what was said:

> MR. MATTINGLY. It's pretty clear that these ESF operations are authorized. I don't think there is a legal problem in terms of the authority. The [ESF] statute is very broadly worded in terms of words like "credit"—**it has covered things like the gold swaps**—and it confers broad authority. [Emphasis added.]

The coming short squeeze. The above, along with a mountain of other evidence, proves that the world's central banks are suppressing gold's exchange rate. But it doesn't explain why they're doing it. Here's why: Because gold is money, it is one of the yardsticks by which the world's currencies—and the central banks that manage them—are measured. When gold's exchange rate is low relative to the dollar and euro, central banks appear to be doing a good job of keeping inflation down and the value of their fiat currencies up. So part of the central banks' motivation has no doubt been to keep exchange rates at favorable levels—by keeping gold undervalued—thus making their currencies and themselves look good.

As for why central-bank manipulation will cause a dramatic spike in gold's exchange rate, let's revisit Chapter 8's explanation of how central banks lend their gold to private-sector bullion banks, which then sell it on the open market. Because the bullion banks have promised to eventually return the borrowed gold to the central banks, they are, in effect, "short" gold. That is, at some point in the future they're obligated to buy gold in order to repay to the central banks. The bullion banks thus benefit when gold is cheap, and are hurt, potentially very seriously, when it rises.

James estimates that central banks have loaned out at least 12,000 tonnes, or about 385.8 million ounces, of their gold. That's almost five times the world's annual gold production, worth about $160 billion at early-2004 exchange rates. If the bullion banks have borrowed this gold at an average of $350 ($11.25/gg), and gold rises to $400 ($12.86/gg) (leaving the euro out of this equation for simplicity), the bullion banks are looking at a loss of $50 times 385.8 million ounces, or $19 billion. If the banks borrowed at $300 ($9.64/gg) on average, they're facing a potential loss of $38 billion, more than enough to bankrupt some of the more aggressive players.

As the cost of acquiring gold begins to rise, the bullion banks—all of which have done the above math—will be tempted to cut their losses by covering their shorts (i.e., buying back their gold) en masse. The result will be a classic "short squeeze," in which everyone tries to buy at once, sending gold's exchange rate through the roof.

Part Four

PROFITING FROM THE DOLLAR'S COLLAPSE

You have to choose between trusting to the natural stability of gold
and the natural stability of the honesty and intelligence of the
members of the Government. And, with due respect for these
gentlemen, I advise you, as long as the capitalist system lasts,
to vote for gold.

—GEORGE BERNARD SHAW

So far, we've focused on the disturbing things that are likely to happen in the coming decade. But the real point of this book is that hard
times, currency crises emphatically included, are hard only if you're
unprepared. Take the right steps now, and the next few years, horrific as
they may be for the average person caught unaware by the dollar's collapse, can be among the most interesting, productive, and, yes, *positive*
of your life. Recall that in the mini-crisis of the 1970s, while most

Americans suffered through what seemed like a dark age of "stagflation," a farsighted few made fortunes in gold, silver, Swiss francs, and oil stocks. But that decade was just a warm-up. This time around, both the dislocations and the opportunities will be much bigger, and the range of choices far wider, making it possible to design a strategy that fits your goals and temperament like a glove.

But in presenting a wide variety of hard-asset-related strategies, we are, in a sense, mixing apples and oranges. So before reading further, make sure you're clear on the distinction between money and investments, or, more specifically, between physical gold and gold-based investments. Bullion coins, gold bars, and digital gold (all of which we'll explain soon) are the metal itself, which can be viewed as liquidity or cash. In other words, gold, in these forms, is money, which you can use to cover your expenses while waiting for the right investment to come along. But this kind of money is not an investment that's likely to "go up" like a house or a stock. Instead, it will hold its value as fiat currencies depreciate. While the price of commodities like oil and wheat are soaring in dollar terms, they'll be more or less stable in gold terms. You'll seem to be "making money" on your gold because its dollar exchange rate will be rising, but in reality you'll be preserving rather than expanding your wealth, holding your ground against the things you must buy to survive. Put another way (just to make this crucial distinction as clear as possible), with physical gold you're storing wealth, avoiding risk, and maintaining liquidity rather than attempting to strike it rich.

Gold-based investments, on the other hand, include gold-mining stocks, related derivatives, and possibly rare coins. They depend for their value on gold's exchange rate, but also on many other things, such as the smooth operation of the U.S. financial markets and the probity, wisdom, and capability of mining-company executives. Chosen well, gold-based investments will go up not just in dollar terms but versus gold itself, allowing you to build capital. But, of course, they can also go down. Investments, in other words, are for expanding but not necessarily storing wealth, and with their upside potential comes the risk of loss. As you go though the following chapters, keep this distinction in mind.

Chapter 13

PHYSICAL GOLD

Since the dawn of recorded history, one of the surest ways to preserve wealth has been to acquire some physical gold, whether in the form of coins, high-karat jewelry, or even raw nuggets, and put it in a safe place. Today, this strategy is as wise as it ever was. But your choices for buying and storing physical gold all have drawbacks that can make them inconvenient. Some better alternatives are coming (as you'll see in Chapter 19's look at twenty-first century gold), but until they're widely available, we're stuck with the traditional ways of owning physical gold.

Yet despite the cost and inconvenience, physical gold, as we said, is a good thing to have, and we recommend that all readers own some. Here's how to select among the current alternatives.

BULLION COINS AND BARS

Gold's already-waning role as currency ended with FDR's 1933 confiscation order. But Americans' interest in it has remained. And as restrictions on owning gold were removed in 1974, mints and refiners began introducing coins and small bars that offered a way to purchase and hold physical gold, otherwise known as bullion.

This trail was blazed by South Africa, which began minting one-ounce gold Krugerrands in 1967 and sold millions of them during the monetary chaos of the 1970s. Since then, several major countries and numerous private mints have entered the business, and bullion is now available in forms ranging from $\frac{1}{10}$-oz. coins to 400-oz. bars, all of which can be ordered online or over the phone and, once delivered, can be held in your hand and/or stored in the safe place of your choosing. Coins like the American Eagle, the Krugerrand, and the Canadian Maple Leaf are known as bullion coins because they're simply gold molded into a familiar shape, with no numismatic, or rarity, value. They might or might not have a "face value," that is, an amount of currency stamped onto them; and they might or might not be "legal tender," that is, official national currency. In any case, their real value depends not on their rarity or country of origin, but on the weight of gold they contain.

In addition to the previously mentioned high-volume coins, it's now possible to build a collection that includes the French Rooster, Chinese Panda, and Austrian Philharmonic, along with bars of various size minted by banks like Credit Suisse and UBS, and refiners like Johnson Matthey. Both coins and bars offer the same attraction: They're gold in a recognizable, portable form, easy to buy, store, and, if necessary, sell (though transaction costs are so high that they're emphatically not trading vehicles). They're yours, to keep in your safe or safe-deposit box or a tin can buried in the backyard, whatever makes you feel safest. They don't depend on anyone else holding up their end of any promise. In short, they're one of the best hedges against humanity's recurring financial crises.

Now let's walk through the process of building a portfolio of physical gold:

Find a good dealer. Unlike, say, U.S. Treasury bills, gold coins and bars aren't normally purchased directly from their source. Instead, national mints and gold refiners sell their coins and bars to dealers, who then tack on a markup and sell them to the public. As in any market, prices and service quality vary among dealers, so finding a trustworthy one is a crucial first step. Ideally, there would be several within a short drive. But in reality, bullion dealers are scarce, and most bullion is bought online or over the phone and delivered through the mail. But just in case, check the Yellow Pages for nearby dealers, and if you find any, visit them to price their bullion, calculating their markups for future reference.

Then check Web-based dealers by Googling "buy gold." You'll turn up dozens of names. But because this business, like most others, is rife with less-than-reputable souls, you'll want to focus on the established dealers whose longevity implies that they've managed to satisfy the bulk of their customers. The table below contains a few such dealers.

But even among the industry leaders, there are vast differences in business practices and specialization. Some sell mostly rare coins, for instance (which are explained in Chapter 16), and offer bullion as more of a courtesy, while others are mainly bullion dealers. Service quality, meanwhile, can vary greatly. So narrow the list by checking with the Better Business Bureau to find out who's been getting complaints and who hasn't. To do this, go to the BBB's Web site—www.bbb.org—and type in the dealer's name (making sure that the search turns up the right company, since there are often others with similar names in different fields). Do this for several dealers and you'll find some wildly varying records of customer complaints and success in resolving them. Obviously, other things being equal, it makes sense to favor the dealers with the cleanest records.

Get the best deal. Once you've cut the dealer list down to a manageable number, visit their Web sites or call them for quotes. You'll notice that, while each marks its coins and bars up from the "spot," or current daily

PRECIOUS-METALS DEALERS

Dealer	Web	Telephone
American Gold Exchange	www.amergold.com	800-613-9323
Blanchard	www.blanchardonline.com	866-550-9093
Investment Rarities	www.investmentrarities.com	800-328-1860
Jefferson Coin & Bullion	www.jeffersoncoinandbullion.com	800-593-2585
Kitco	www.kitco.com	877-775-4826
USA Gold	www.usagold.com	800-869-5115

exchange rate, the size of the markup varies. The table below lists the prices for some representative coins and bars from various dealers in early 2004, when the spot quote for gold was $412.90.

Choose the right kind of bullion. The menu, as we noted earlier, includes well-known, highly popular coins produced by the U.S., Canada, and South Africa, obscure-but-fascinating coins from distant corners of the globe, and bars from banks and refiners. They range in size from coins smaller than a dime to bars the size of masonry bricks. Which is best for you depends on your needs and goals, but here's what you'll want to consider:

Weight. It costs just as much to fabricate a $1/4$-ounce coin as a larger one, so higher-weight coins tend to offer more gold for your money. Large bars, meanwhile, are typically cheaper to make than coins and so tend to sell at the lowest markup, followed by one-ounce coins and then by smaller coins.

Type of coin or bar. Common bullion coins are easy to sell because they're instantly recognized and accepted, while bars are a little trickier. In many

Gold Coins and Bars		U.S. $ Prices 1/20/04	
	Kitco	American Gold Exchange	Jefferson Coin & Bullion
Gold Eagle, 1 oz. *	$434.66	434.25	432.00
Canadian Maple Leaf, 1 oz. *	$432.60	432.50	428.50
South African Krugerrand, 1 oz. *	$420.24	424.75	422.0
Gold bar, 1 oz.	$424.00	NA	430.0
Gold bar, 10 oz.	$4,242.00	NA	NA
Gold bar, 100 gr.	NA	NA	NA
Gold bar, kilo	$13,422.93	NA	NA
Spot gold/oz.	**412.90**		

* Price for orders of ten or more coins

cases, you'll have to have a gold bar assayed before you can sell it, in order to prove that it's not just gold-plated lead. This lack of universal acceptance is a drawback if you're planning to buy and sell your bullion frequently. But if you're going to store it for a long time (which you should), then selling becomes less of an issue. So if the objective is to get the most gold for your money, then the answer is simple: Buy the biggest bar you can afford. Hundred-gram bars (at 31.1034 grams per troy ounce) weigh a little more than three ounces and are a good, cost-effective choice. As the table on page 96 illustrates, however, they aren't yet widely available.

If you're willing to pay a little extra for the familiarity and wide acceptance of coins, the one-ounce versions tend to carry the most reasonable (relatively speaking) markup. Another thing you'll notice when you begin researching coins is that some are more "pure" than others. The Austrian Philharmonic, for instance, claims to be 99.99 percent pure, while the Gold Eagle is only 91.67 percent. This is deceptive, because it doesn't refer to the amount of gold in the coin: Both begin with a full ounce. Instead, purity refers to the amount of other metals—usually copper or other base metals—that are added during the smelting process to make the coins harder, the better to withstand the wear and tear of their existence. This makes the Gold Eagle a little harder and heavier, but since you're planning to put the coins in a safe place and leave them there, purity isn't an important issue.

Place your order. Once you know what you want, call some dealers or visit their Web sites and nail down their prices for the package of bullion you've chosen. Bullion dealers aren't usually able to accept online orders, so expect to confirm your order over the phone. The person at the other end will be able to "lock in" the price at the time you place your order, as well as explain whatever special deals are available. Perhaps they're offering preselected portfolios of gold coins for a set price, or a slight discount on some overstocked coin, or free shipping on orders over a certain size. You'll want to be very clear about all this to calculate the best deal.

To finalize the order, you'll either give a credit-card number (not to pay for the coins, but to cover the dealer if the price of gold declines and they never receive your payment) or send a check or bank wire. Once they've been paid, they'll send you the gold via registered mail, for which you'll have to sign, or move the gold into allocated storage, which we'll explain below. How can you be sure that you'll actually get what you've ordered (or anything at all)? That's a very good question and brings us back to the first bit of advice in this chapter: By dealing with reputable companies that have been keeping their promises for years, you ensure that you'll get what you pay for.

Store your gold. With bars, it's often simpler to have the dealer or some other fiduciary store them for you, thus preserving the "chain of integrity" and making the bars easier to sell. Coins, being widely recognized and accepted, are more convenient to hold on to. Each choice is a little tricky, however, with risks that aren't always apparent going in, so we'll go over them in some detail here. If you're going to have someone else store your gold for you, be sure to understand the following distinctions:

Unallocated vs. allocated. These are the two most basic methods of storage. When you store on an allocated basis, you continue to own the gold. There is no transfer of title. You deliver gold bars to the fiduciary's vault under a contractual agreement that the exact same bars will be returned to you upon request. The content of the vault is insured by a rock-solid third party (that's something you'll want to verify), so that even if the vault is robbed or swallowed by an earthquake or whatever, you'll get your gold or its equivalent value. In return for this service, you pay an annual storage fee of one or two percent of your gold's value.

With unallocated gold you give your money to a bullion bank, which promises to give you back a certain amount of gold on request—though not any particular piece of gold. You've thus become an unsecured creditor of the bullion bank, which puts you at risk if the bank—as many will in the coming decade—becomes insolvent. So if you hire a company to store your gold, it should be allocated.

Pool account. This is an account in which your gold is commingled with the gold of other people (which is easy to do because gold is a fungible commodity). The resulting economies of scale allow the company offering the pooling account to keep its fees nice and low. Pooled gold can be allocated and unallocated. If the former, the customers in the pool collectively own specific gold bars. In most pooling arrangements, however, the gold is unallocated, meaning that you are, in effect, loaning your money to the bank or dealer running the pool. As we said, this is a bad deal; don't do it.

Gold certificates. These certificates are common and are perhaps the most misunderstood type of storage, because they aren't storage at all. A gold certificate is simply a promise of gold in the future, which is the basic nature of any "certificate." Say, for instance, that you deposit dollars with your neighborhood bank. As evidence of the transaction, the bank gives you a "certificate of deposit." You no longer own the money. Instead, you've become an unsecured general creditor of the bank. Gold certificates work the same way. Instead of owning the gold, you are an unsecured general creditor of the bank, trading firm, or mint that issued you the certificate. Like an unallocated pool account, this is emphatically not the same thing as owning gold, and we don't recommend it.

Self-storing gold. Now let's say that instead of allowing someone else to store your gold, you've opted to take delivery. The big day arrives, and there you are, gathered around the kitchen table gawking at a box of shining gold bars and/or coins. What now? You can't leave them in a kitchen drawer, any more than you would a roll of twenties. A good home safe is a more logical possibility, though these advertise the location of your wealth to intruders and can be simply carried away by a couple of strong men. So if you choose this option, be sure to hide your safe and/or make it completely immobile. Another possibility is a bank safe-deposit box, which can be rented for a few dollars a year and is very seldom disturbed. These are not, however, absolutely safe, so be sure to buy insurance, either as a rider on your homeowner's policy or through the bank itself. And note that should a rapacious future government choose to once again confiscate its citizens' gold, your safe-deposit box can be frozen with the stroke of a pen.

Or you can just hide your coins in a place known only to you. Gold doesn't tarnish, so you can (and many people do) literally bury it in the backyard. Or you can divide your bullion into several caches, putting some in a safe and some under a loose floorboard. Just be sure to remember what you've done! And because you don't want to take this secret to your grave, leave a treasure map with your lawyer or a trusted friend.

How to sell. When it comes time to spend your gold, reverse the above process. Find the reputable dealer that offers the best price. You might receive a little less than spot (the difference is how dealers make money), but if the world goes the way we expect, you won't quibble about a few dollars.

Chapter 14

GOLD IN THE GROUND:

MINING STOCKS

The most lucrative way to profit from gold's revival is to buy the shares of companies that mine it. For reasons we'll explain in a minute, mining shares tend to appreciate even faster than gold itself. Like any other kind of stock, they're easy to buy and sell. They don't require any special storage or insurance and often pay dividends, in some cases at two or three times the rate of today's money market funds. And this is an extraordinary time to own them, because, like gold itself, mining shares have rarity value.

The number of major gold mines in the world is limited, and after 4,000 years of searching it's unlikely that we'll suddenly find a whole lot more. And in the wake of gold's two-decade-long bear market, the gold-mining sector is tiny. Despite a nice recent comeback from their 2000 lows, by late 2003 the market capitalization of all the gold mining stocks in the world was something like $100 billion, which was about a third of Microsoft's market value and less than 2 percent of the combined values of the companies making up the S&P 500 Index. The market cap of Newmont Mining, the largest gold miner in the world and the only gold miner in the S&P 500, was only $17.6 billion.

When money really starts flowing into this sector, we'll see price moves reminiscent of tech stocks circa 1999. But—and we want to make this point absolutely clear—this does not mean you should buy a random assortment of gold-mining stocks and forget about them. Like any other sector, gold mining has its good and bad apples, steady growers and lottery tickets. And all of them, once bought, have to be monitored. So to really benefit from the coming super bull market in this sector, you'll want to build a portfolio that fits your means and temperament.

This chapter will show you how, but first, a brief warning: Analyzing gold miners and their shares is not simple, and some of the topics covered here are a little heavy on mining and accounting jargon. So if you find yourself getting bogged down, feel free to skip ahead and come back when you're ready for more information.

GOLD MINING 101

Before you can decide whether a given gold-mining stock is a good investment, it helps to understand how the business works. So let's begin at the beginning, which for our purposes is about three billion years ago, when submicroscopic bits of a heavy element we now call gold settled into deposits of quartz and sulfides, in concentrations ranging from several grams to, in rare instances, hundreds of grams per ton of surrounding material. Eventually, the sulfides began to break down and their gold was released, in some cases coalescing into the veins that have come to play such a notable role in human history. Once formed, these veins experience several fates: Some, either near the surface when created or elevated by tectonic activity, are exposed to the elements and the surrounding minerals are eroded away, exposing the gold. This is often washed into riverbeds to form "alluvial" deposits consisting of gold fragments ranging from dust to nuggets. (The world's largest recorded nugget, by the way, is "the Welcome Stranger." Discovered in Australia in 1869, it weighs 2,284 ounces, or 71.04 kilos, and is nearly two feet long.) The rest of the world's gold stays hidden deep in the earth until some enterprising miner or geologist finds it.

When gold is discovered, the next step is to get at it, and there are generally two large-scale ways of doing this. If the gold is near the surface, the solution is an open-pit mine, basically a huge strip mine in which earthmovers scoop up the ore-bearing rock for processing. If it's underground, miners dig long shafts that follow the ore vein. And we do mean long. Some South African mines extend more than 5,000 meters below ground, and the tunnels dug horizontally from these shafts stretch for miles into the surrounding bedrock. Depending on the level of capital employed, deep-shaft miners either break up the gold seams with picks or use massive drilling machines and large amounts of dynamite. The resulting rubble is brought to the surface, loaded onto conveyor belts or rail cars, and transported to the mine's onsite processing plant.

Mined ore is ground into a powder and mixed into a solution of cyanide and other chemicals, which attach to minute particles of gold to form a water-soluble, gold-cyanide compound from which the gold can later be recovered. Invented in 1887 in Scotland and perfected in the 1960s by the U.S. Bureau of Mines, "heap leaching" was a huge advance in mining technology and now makes it possible to extract just about all the gold, even the microscopic particles, from a pile of ore.

This onsite processing results in "dore bars," generally containing 60–80 percent gold. They are shipped to refiners, which apply processes like "Miller chlorination" or "Wohlwill electrolytic" to remove the remaining impurities. The resulting nearly-pure gold is shaped into "ingots" (i.e., bars ranging from less than one kilo to 400 ounces) and sold to dealers, who in turn supply the jewelry, electronics, and coinage markets.

There are hundreds of gold mines operating in the world at any given time, ranging from the barely functional to behemoths like Freeport McMoran's Grasberg mine in Indonesia, which produces more than 2,000,000 ounces (62 tonnes) each year. Mines now operate on virtually every major landmass, though gold deposits seem to be more common in places like South Africa (which has produced about a third of today's aboveground stock of gold) and North America, and less common in Europe.

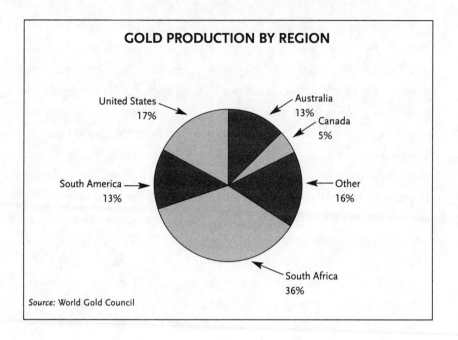

GOLD PRODUCTION BY REGION

United States 17%
Australia 13%
Canada 5%
South America 13%
Other 16%
South Africa 36%

Source: World Gold Council

ANALYZING THE MINERS

Armed with a general sense of how miners do their thing, let's look at how they differ. And do they ever differ. In this forest there are elephants and mice—and lots of tigers. Here's how to tell them apart:

Size matters. Mining companies exist on a pretty much continuous spectrum from tiny to huge, but here we'll divide them into five groups within two broad categories. The first category contains the companies that are currently producing gold—in other words, the actual miners—which are known as majors, mid-tiers, and juniors, depending on the amount of gold they produce. The second category contains the nonproducers: the exploration companies that hope to make new gold discoveries, and the development companies whose aim is to turn economic ore bodies into working mines. Let's call these two groups "property plays."

Gold producers. The majors are the big players, managing vast portfolios of mines throughout the world that together produce several million ounces each year. They've generally been created by aggressive management teams that bought up smaller companies and individual properties and did a great job of melding them into an efficient whole. The biggest—and arguably best managed—of the majors is Newmont Mining, which over the past decade has acquired sizable operators like Santa Fe Pacific Gold, Battle Mountain Gold, and Normandy Mining, while developing its existing properties into prolific mines. It now brings to market about 7,000,000 ounces each year, worth about $2.8 billion at $400/oz. ($12.86/gg).

Generally, the majors are followed by many analysts and money managers, and widely held by investors. They tend to be mentioned frequently in media accounts of gold's exchange rate or the performance of gold shares. Because of this visibility, they, like IBM and Microsoft, usually trade efficiently. That is, all the information that's publicly available is quickly disseminated to the world's trading desks and media outlets, so that their market values at any given time reflect a broad consensus of savvy investors. Buy a stock like Newmont, Gold Fields, or Harmony, and you're betting that the price of gold will rise by more than the investment community expects, but not that the company possesses strengths unknown to the rest of the world. Put another way, while majors frequently get lucky with a new discovery, you don't buy a major anticipating appreciation in its stock price from the results of its "green fields" exploration. You buy it because of its cash flow, and management's ability to generate attractive returns on its capital from proficient mining and a rising gold price.

Mid-tiers and juniors are established miners that operate anywhere from one to a handful of producing mines. Glamis Gold, for example, owns mines in the U.S. and Honduras, which together yield 250,000 ounces a year, and has new mines coming onstream soon in Guatemala and Mexico that could in a few years double its production. Mid-tiers, especially young ones, tend to be less visible to the investing public, because they're not big enough (in terms of market capitalization and circulating shares, or "float") to attract the attention of large numbers of analysts, reporters, or money managers. So it's possible for a mid-tier to bring a promising new property online without much fanfare, and to generate the occasional very big, very pleasant surprise. Glamis, for instance, languished at less than $2 a share in the late 1990s, when gold was weak and investors were largely unaware that the company was developing some potentially big properties. But in January 2001 its low-cost Marigold, Nevada, mine began producing, and the investment community began to crunch the resulting numbers. In the following two years, Glamis's stock soared in one beautiful arc from $1.50 to $15.

This small-to-big transition is more common than you might think. The market for gold stocks is very narrow, with few analysts bothering to look beyond the majors and leading mid-tiers, and few investors willing to take a flyer on a high-risk business they don't understand or value. As a result, mid-tiers and juniors offer an interesting mix of traits. They are going concerns, with production and revenues, and frequently a promising new project pipeline. But they're often overlooked by the investment community at large, making it possible, with a little digging, to find gems like Glamis circa 2000 just waiting to be scooped up. The table that follows illustrates the money that was made in some of the more successful mid-tiers and juniors while gold was rising from $272 to $415. Imagine how this kind of list will look after gold hits $1,000.

SUCCESSFUL MID-TIER AND JUNIOR GOLD-MINING STOCKS

Company	Ticker Symbol	$ Price 1/1/01	$ Price 12/31/03	% Change
Golden Star Resources	GSS	0.90	6.97	574
Glamis Gold	GLG	1.36	11.37	762
Meridian Gold	MDG	6.27	15.60	149
Eldorado Gold	EGO	1.52*	3.25	113
Gold		272/oz. ($8.75/gg)	415/oz. ($13.34/gg)	**52**
S&P 500		1366	1114	−23

* Price on first day of AMEX listing, January 24, 2003

Property plays. Exploration and development companies are not technically miners, because they don't operate functioning mines. But they hope to one day, in the process making themselves and their investors rich.

Explorers, as the name implies, are in the business of looking for deposits that might become working gold mines. Their exploration strategies vary, but frequently they focus on areas where other gold mines are located, on the assumption that "the neighborhood" is likely to contain other, as yet undiscovered, deposits. Sometimes they re-analyze old workings that were inadequately explored in the past. In any event, the right geology is the key. There's a lot of exploration in Nevada, for instance, where the earth contains many deposits, and very little exploration in Illinois, where, so far at least, gold has not been discovered.

Development companies, meanwhile, may have a property with indications of some mineralization, which they hope to develop into a working mine. They conduct extensive drilling to "prove up" the size of the resource, and feasibility studies to determine if the ore can be mined profitably. If the results are positive, they then develop the property by building roads, digging shafts or a pit, setting up power generators, and doing whatever else is necessary to make the resource minable.

Exploration and development companies are the lottery tickets of the mining world, and when they succeed, they frequently make their investors very rich. Canadian-based Francisco Gold, to take one of many possible examples, labored in near-total obscurity for several years in the late 1990s, developing a promising property in Mexico. It was run by a veteran team that had acquired the exploration rights for a song and had attracted considerable outside capital. By 1999, Francisco had about US$2.50 a share in cash on hand, no debt, gold in the ground worth between $10 and $15 a share, and a stock price of about $2. And outside the company, the only people aware of the situation were gold-stock newsletter writers like *The OrMetal Report*'s Claude Cormier, who was telling anyone who would listen that this was his favorite emerging miner.

As drilling results revealed increasing amounts of gold, and as management brought the mine closer to operation, Francisco's share price

began to creep up, but by the beginning of 2002 it was still only about
$3.50. The handful of investors who took the plunge at this point didn't
have to wait long for their payoff, which came in the form of a March
2002 buyout by Glamis for $13 per share.

But we used the term "lottery ticket" for a reason. Exploration and
development companies depend less on the exchange rate of gold soaring (which is what drives the values of majors and to a great extent mid-
tiers and juniors) than on their ability to turn a piece of raw land into a
profitable mine. So profiting in this segment of the market is a very different game, in which an understanding of the "macro" monetary debasement that makes gold so attractive is less important than the ability
to read and understand drilling results and judge the quality of management (more about these skills shortly). And keep in mind that for every
moonshot like Francisco Gold, there are hundreds of exploration companies that, no matter how well qualified their CEOs or solid their
finances, will never make a discovery. That's the cold, hard fact of gold
exploration, so don't lose sight of the high risks if you decide to expand
your portfolio by adding some property plays.

GOLD MINERS: BIG, SMALL, AND IN BETWEEN

	Property Play	Mid-tier	Major
Company/ Ticker Symbol	Nevsun/NSU.TO	Glamis/GLG	Newmont/NEM
2003 Gold production ounces	0	252,000	7,300,000
Proven/probable reserves (mill. oz.)	0	4.9	88
Annual revenues ($ millions)	0	83	3,340
Shares outstanding (millions)	73.80	129.84	403.70
Market Cap ($ millions)	265	2,200	17,640
Analyst coverage	5	16	25

All figures as of 12/31/03

Source: Company annual reports, Yahoo! Finance

Judging the quality of a miner's properties. In gold mining, like any other business, size is just part of the story. Profit and market value, which of course are the ultimate goals, depend on how much it costs to produce each gram of gold, and how long the resulting earnings stream lasts. So to really understand a miner, you have to be able to assess the quality of its properties. And that means developing a firm grasp of the following:

Size of the deposit. The single most important number is how much gold the mine contains. But since the gold is scattered among millions of tons of underground rock, there's no way, before actually digging it up, to say with certainty how much is there. So a miner develops an estimate of the shape, scope, and quality of an ore body by drilling a series of holes and analyzing what it pulls up. If drill results and geological modeling indicate a million tons of ore, and each ton contains one ounce of gold, then the company will announce that its "proven" reserves are 1,000,000 ounces. For a deposit to be "proven," drilling must be tightly and regularly spaced, in most cases no more than fifty to seventy-five feet apart. When drilled, these properties look like a punchboard with neatly spaced drill holes.

"Probable reserves," meanwhile, is a much easier standard to meet, with less drilling and more reliance on geological modeling. One useful measure of the accuracy of a miner's testing is the rate at which its probable reserves turn into proven reserves over time. A high rate implies that the deposit fits neatly into the geological model developed for it, while a low rate implies an irregular, unpredictable deposit that might produce less gold than originally thought.

Ore quality. Some ore bodies contain much more gold than others, and a tonne of rich ore obviously produces more gold than a tonne of low-quality ore. The term for this is "grade," and it is usually presented metrically in terms of grams of gold per tonne of ore (though some North American miners with a traditionalist bent still report in ounces per ton). Right now, some mines can work with ore containing less than 1 gram of gold per tonne, though the highest-quality deposits—like

Goldcorp's Red Lake mine, which contains about 65 grams per tonne—
are obviously a lot more profitable to exploit.

Cost. In a nutshell, if gold is $400 an ounce ($12.86/gg), a miner can
get rich producing it for $200 an ounce ($6.43/gg) and go broke producing for $450 ($14.46/gg). Ore quality is obviously one key to this
calculation, but other things come into play as well, including:

- How hard is it to get at the ore? If it's sitting a few inches below the
  wildflowers in a local meadow, then the cost of creating and running
  a mine is considerably less than if it's 3,000 meters belowground and
  hundreds of miles away from basic infrastructure like roads and electricity. So generally speaking, an open-pit mine in an accessible place
  is a lower-cost proposition than a deep-shaft mine in the hinterlands.
  But, of course, it's seldom that simple. Open-pit mines move a lot
  more dirt than underground mines, lessening their cost advantage.
  And ore is rarely just sitting there at the surface. More often, the
  shape of the ore body is irregular, leading to deep, oddly shaped pits
  requiring a lot of expensive excavation. A miner takes these factors
  into account when estimating a mine's cash cost of production.
- Ore production levels. The more ore a mine can process each day—
  known as throughput—the greater the economies of scale available
  to its operator, and the lower the cost of obtaining each gram of
  gold. This number depends on both the geology of the mine and the
  amount of capital a miner has devoted to create capacity. Because
  miners strive for efficient returns, not volume, the average mine
  produces at a lower output level than it could if all possible equipment was used on the deposit.
- Other minerals. Useful minerals are sometimes mixed together
  in the earth, so occasionally the rocks coming out of a gold mine
  will hold silver, zinc, or copper, among other things. These can be
  extracted and smelted along with the gold, lowering the cash cost of
  gold extraction. Toronto-based Agnico-Eagle's LaRonde mine, for
  instance, produces silver, copper, and zinc as by-products. Even its

name—Ag Ni Company, with Ag and Ni standing for silver and nickel—reflects its polymetallic past. Without the by-products, its 2003 cash cost was $250 per ounce (8.04/gg) of gold; with them, the cost dropped to $155 (4.98/gg). Meanwhile, the largest silver mine in the world—Cannington in Australia—is actually a copper mine that produces silver as a by-product.

Add it all up—throughput, ore quality, and accessibility—and you get the cost of extraction. At the low-cost end of the spectrum are operations like Goldcorp's underground but high-grade Red Lake mine in northwestern Ontario, at about $65/oz. ($2.09/gg). At the other end of the spectrum is AngloGold's South African Joel deposit, with costs of $345/oz. ($11.09/gg), with the average for the world's major gold producers in the neighborhood of $180/oz. ($5.79/gg).

But note that "cash" production costs are just part of the miner's cost structure. To determine an operator's profitability, its other expenses, including administration (i.e., salaries and general overhead), interest, and depreciation have to be added in. We'll explain these costs a few pages ahead.

Expansion potential. It takes years, sometimes decades, to fully explore a rich ore body, and it's not worthwhile for a miner to discover more reserves than it can profitably extract in a reasonable time. So many properties contain more ore than the "proven and probable" number would indicate, often much more. The industry refers to these hoped-for deposits with terms like "unproven and probable mineralization" and "indicated and inferred reserves." As these terms imply, the existence of this ore hasn't been unequivocally proved, though the figure is generally based on some level of testing and geological modeling and often turns out to be real. Goldcorp, for instance, estimates its mineralization at 5.5 million ounces. Newmont's figure is nearly 55 million ounces, and some of the South African mines have indicated and inferred resources over 100 million. As you'll see in the next section, the difference between overvalued and undervalued can be these as-yet-unproven reserves.

Valuing reserves. Once you understand the quality and size of a miner's properties, the next step is to figure out what they're worth, and compare the result to the current share price. This, unfortunately, isn't easy, since gold mines aren't like other businesses. Whereas a factory or store can be valued on the earnings and/or cash flow it generates, the value of a mining property is derived in large part from what it contains rather than what it is currently producing. Operating mines normally have much more gold in the ground than they extract in a given year, and, as you know, varying levels of potential additional reserves.

When gold's exchange rate changes, the market revalues a miner's entire resource base, making gold-mining shares far more volatile than gold itself. So a mining stock is, in a sense, a gold derivative—that is, an option on the future depreciation of the dollar.

How do you calculate a gold miner's value? One very good method comes courtesy of William Fleckenstein, short seller extraordinaire and articulate precious-metals bull. Using Newmont Mining as our example, begin with the company's proven and probable reserves, which at the end of 2003 were about 88 million ounces. Then divide the company's early 2004 market value of $17.4 billion into this number, and the result—$198—is what you pay per ounce for these reserves when you buy the stock. Next, add in Newmont's cash production cost of about $200 an ounce, and you're paying, in effect, $398 per ounce for the gold that Newmont is likely to produce. Toss in its noncash costs (headquarters salaries, depreciation and exploration costs) of $60 an ounce and your cost rises to $458. With gold at $415 an ounce, this isn't an especially compelling deal so far.

But recall that proven and probable reserves aren't all you get with a gold miner. In addition to the 88 million ounces that are almost certainly there, Newmont has another 55 million ounces of "mineralization" that might one day be shifted over to the proven category. Add these to the 88 million, and you get a total of 143 million ounces. Assume that each of these ounces costs $200 to extract and add in the noncash costs of $60/oz., and the cost per ounce for Newmont stock drops to $382. The conclusion: At its year-end 2003 price, this stock is

CALCULATING THE VALUE OF NEWMONT'S GOLD

Proven and probable reserves

Proven and probable reserves (million ounces)	88.0	
Market value of outstanding shares at 12/31/03 ($ billions)	17.4	
Market value of proven and probable reserves, $/oz.		198
Cash mining costs, $/oz.	200	
Noncash costs, $/oz.	60	
Shareholders' cost per ounce of proven and probable reserves, $/oz.		458

Total gold in the ground

Proven and probable reserves (million ounces)	88.0	
Mineralization (million ounces)	55.0	
Total gold in the ground (million ounces)	143	
Market value of gold in the ground, $/oz.		122
Cash mining cost, $/oz.	200	
Noncash costs, $/oz.	60	
Shareholders' cost per ounce of proven and probable reserves, $/oz.		382

Source: Newmont annual report, Yahoo! Finance

a buy with gold at $415 an ounce, and a screaming buy if you assume, as we do, that gold is going much higher.

Other considerations. After you've placed a value on a miner's reserves, consider the other factors that affect the value of its gold deposits. Among them:

Country risk. If a miner has one property in a small, politically unstable country, its output is less dependable and therefore less valuable than a mine in, say, North America. That's why U.S. and Canadian mining stocks tend to trade at higher multiples of earnings, cash flow, and reserves than do South African or Latin American miners. Especially for those companies with a limited number of properties, location is something to watch closely.

Mine type. Not to pick on South Africa, but those deep deposits present some incredible engineering challenges. Let a shaft collapse at 3,000 meters, and you won't be seeing any gold for a while. Open-pit mines like Freeport's giant Grasberg mine are generally more stable, since they're sitting on the surface, but even they are not immune to acts of God. Torrential rain, for instance, can cause pit walls to give way. Engineering, whether above- or belowground, has limits, and mining as a result is a hazardous occupation with real, and occasionally deadly, risks. In short, it's hard to make generalizations about which types of mines are more or less risky, but still useful to know the trade-offs between open-pit and deep-shaft.

Diversification. Owning a single great mine is a nice, relatively simple way to make a fortune. That is, until something goes wrong. Agnico-Eagle investors discovered this hard fact in 2003, when a cave-in at its flagship LaRonde mine cut production for several months. This sudden interruption of what had been a steady earnings stream spooked Agnico-Eagle's investors, who sliced 40 percent from its stock price after the collapse. The lesson: A portfolio of mines in different places is less prone to disruption—whether operational or political—than a single all-important property. Newmont, at the opposite extreme, has "core" properties on four continents, with a fifth on the way.

Environmental issues. Cyanide leaching was a godsend for miners, making it possible to extract even microscopic quantities of gold from ore that in earlier decades would've been worthless. But cyanide is a poison, and though in general the mining industry's environmental record is good, the result of sloppy mining practices has been devastating in certain high-profile cases. As a result, concerns about environmental risks are leading to conflicts between mine operators and local people and governments, which in turn raises costs, lowers production, and occasionally prevents otherwise-promising properties from being developed. So a company's environmental record and its relationship with its neighbors are crucial parts of the reserve quality puzzle.

These risks are spelled out in company 10-K reports under footnote headings like "litigation" and "environmental issues." But it pays to look beyond company documents. A Google search under "Newmont gold environmental" in October 2003, for instance, turned up dozens of entries, with titles like "Newmont CEO Parries Environmental Attacks at Shareholder Meeting," "Peruvian Campesinos Fight Newmont Gold Mine," and "Las Vegas SUN: Environmentalists Try to Block Newmont Gold Mining." The location of a mine, in short, often limits the ability of its owner to expand and operate it. And really understanding the assets of a given miner means having a general sense of how environmental laws and their interpretation are affecting its main properties. Here again, diversification is a huge plus, because it lessens the impact of potential environmental snags at any one mine.

The new mine pipeline. At least one prominent historian has likened gold to a drug, which throughout history has led those addicted to it to do both extraordinary and appalling things. So let's extend that analogy a little and note that in a very important sense, miners are like drug companies. The way Merck and Pfizer are constantly developing and testing new compounds, miners are constantly exploring, sizing up, and bringing new properties online. As you'll recall from the earlier example of Glamis, a big new mine, like a blockbuster drug, can be the key to a junior's emergence. Or it can allow a major to replenish its reserves. Meanwhile, the opposite is also true: Like a drug company whose stock drops when a promising drug fails in clinical trials, a mining company suffers when a new mine doesn't pan out. Up-and-coming mid-tier Meridian, for example, saw its stock fall about 50 percent in early 2003 (when gold's exchange rate was rising), after local protests forced it to halt development of its promising Esquel property in Argentina.

When a miner's drilling reveals something of value, or when those drill results reveal nothing, which is also important, it generally releases the results. These releases, like the details of a clinical drug trial, can be hard to decipher but are potentially great sources of clues to the future.

Revenue policy. Now that you have a handle on the physical side of gold mining, let's look at its financial side. That is, where does a miner get its capital, and how does the company use it to build and run its mine portfolio? There are several ways for a miner to turn metal into cash, and its choices say a lot about both its management philosophy and its prospects in gold's bull market. Here, the industry can be divided into three broad camps:

Hedged. The jewelry makers and electronics firms that use gold know more or less how much they'll need over the next year. What they don't know is how much the gold will cost. If prices spike, their costs might rise to levels that make it impossible to sell their products profitably. As a result, they're willing to pay a little extra to lock in their future gold supplies.

Gold miners face the opposite problem. They know what they'll produce over the coming year and at what cost but worry that prices might fall, wiping out their profit margins. So the various players in the gold market often cut deals in which they agree to buy or sell a given amount of gold at a given price months or years in advance.

This is known as hedging (as in "hedging your bets"), and for a miner, it locks in a profit, at the cost of forgone gains if gold surges. Not an unreasonable thing on its face, and quite smart when gold's exchange rate is falling, as it did in the late 1990s. Since the "forward price" for gold is always higher than the spot market (a configuration called "contango"), a company that hedges its production will receive a higher average price than its peers in an environment where gold's exchange rate is flat or falling but earn less than its unhedged peers when gold is rising by more than the contango.

In the beginning, hedging was—and still is for most miners—as we've described it here, a logical, seemingly harmless tool for locking in profits and avoiding the risk of wild price swings. But over the past few years, some of the major hedgers, with Barrick leading the way, began to treat their hedge books like a line of credit, selling future output today and using the proceeds to develop new mines or generate interest income. At its peak, this off-balance-sheet leverage was sky-high. Barrick's year-end 2002 hedge book of 24 million ounces was equivalent to more than one-fifth of the world's annual gold production.

Barrick's hedges are of a type known as "spot-deferred," which means that the delivery obligation they incur can be deferred into the future. Say, for instance, that Barrick has contracted to supply a million ounces at $340 ($10.93/gg) but the spot market goes to $375 ($12.06/gg). Under the terms of its spot-deferred hedge, Barrick can simply sell the gold it was prepared to deliver under the $340 contract directly into the market for $375. Its obligation to deliver gold at $340 is put off for another day, with the only downside being a decline in the marked-to-market value of its hedge book, an off-balance-sheet entry that doesn't affect earnings. Its income statement, meanwhile, shows a big profit from those spot-market gold sales.

Hedging on this scale made Barrick, by its own calculations, an extra $2 billion in the 1990s. But most of this gain was given back over the past few years as gold recovered. In any event, hedging that extends more than one year (and Barrick goes out more than ten years in some cases) is arguably no longer hedging. It is borrowing and should be analyzed like any other debt on the company's balance sheet. Viewed this way, Barrick's hedging profits have come with a very high price tag, in the form of obligations to provide millions of ounces of gold at exchange rates that in our view will more than likely be far below future spot levels.

Under pressure from bankers terrified of the company's mounting liabilities (or perhaps because it was losing the pretrial maneuvering in a suit brought by gold dealer Blanchard, alleging manipulation of the gold market), Barrick threw in the towel in late 2003, announcing an end to its hedging program. By year-end its hedge book had shrunk from 24 million ounces to 15.5 million.

To sum up, hedging—on a modest scale and with a six- to twelve-month time horizon—can be a smart move when gold is falling and reckless when it's rising. And since we expect gold not just to rise but to surge, the hedgers as a group are best avoided.

Unhedged. These miners refine gold and sell it, for whatever the market offers. Obviously, when gold is down they don't do as well as their hedged

competitors, and when it's up they do better. The biggest and most vocif-
erous of the unhedged majors is Newmont. After buying Australian
major—and big hedger—Normandy in 2002, Newmont had a chance to
live up to its ideals, and did so, eliminating its inherited 9-million-ounce
hedge book within eighteen months, at an opportunity cost of nearly
$200 million. In other words, had Normandy not been hedged, New-
mont would have generated an additional $200 million from its gold
sales.

Holders. The third and most aggressive method of turning gold into cash
is not doing it at all, by holding on to some of each year's gold production. The effect is to place an even bigger bet on gold versus the dollar.
And (this won't surprise you) we think it's a brilliant strategy. The two
biggest holders are Goldcorp and IAMGOLD. As of September 30,
2003, for instance, Goldcorp held 266,730 ounces, or about 30 percent
more than the Bank of Canada. Then, at year-end, it sold its hoard at a
big profit, declared a large cash dividend, and began accumulating gold
once again. We love these guys!

Leverage. Now let's consider the relationship between a company's
earnings and gold's exchange rate. In other words, how much extra
profit does a miner generate when gold rises by X amount, and what
kinds of risk does it incur to achieve these gains? The general term for
this concept is leverage, and it comes in several flavors:

Financial leverage. Developing a gold mine is a lot like building a factory,
in that one of the first and most important decisions is how and on what
terms to acquire the necessary capital. You can borrow some national
currency, for instance, which saddles you with ongoing interest costs
but allows you to keep whatever profit you generate. You can, like
Barrick in the previous section, employ "gold financing" by borrowing
against and selling your production ahead of time. Similarly, you can
contract for a "net smelter royalty" by agreeing to pay your financiers a
percentage of the mine's revenue.

You can issue equity, which is selling a part of the company to out-side investors, either privately or through a public stock offering. This avoids onerous interest costs but requires that you share future profits, and possible control, with your new part-owners. Or you can generate the needed cash from your current operations, which has none of the drawbacks of debt or equity, but can be slow, because you probably aren't throwing off anything like the amount of money you could raise externally with the stroke of a pen.

Each of the above strategies has its advantages and is being employed, individually or in combination, by well-run miners. The differences show up in the miners' balances sheets, where financially leveraged miners carry a lot of debt in relation to the capital they've acquired by other means. It also affects their income statements, where they earn less because of their interest charges but spread what's left over fewer shares of stock.

Why should you care about a mining company's balance sheet? Because it affects the miner's risk profile, as well as its earnings and mar-ket value. In hard times, which for our purposes are defined as a declining gold exchange rate, mining profits fall, and a producer with too much debt may have trouble covering its interest expense. In cases like this, the producer's lenders have the power to take over the company and do what-ever's necessary to get their money back, potentially leaving shareholders with nothing. Debt-free companies don't have this problem. Their share-holders may not do as well when gold falls, of course, but the company's survival isn't threatened by angry creditors. Hedged miners, meanwhile, tend to outperform their unhedged peers in down markets.

When gold's exchange rate is rising, on the other hand, financial leverage (i.e., a lot of fiat-currency debt) can be a plus, because the bur-den of the debt—denominated in a depreciating currency—is declin-ing. The result is faster increases in earnings, less anxiety about interest costs, and more investor enthusiasm for the stock.

Operating leverage. Low-cost mines tend to be more profitable and of course are less at risk in a falling-gold-price environment, so their owners are generally seen as the stars of the industry and tend to have higher market values at any given time. But in a rising gold environment, high-cost miners actually have an advantage. Since their profit margins are relatively narrow to begin with, a rising gold exchange rate gives them a bigger percentage boost than their lower-cost cousins. To illustrate, let's take two hypothetical miners, both of which produce one million ounces per year. Company A, a low-cost producer able to bring gold to market for $150 per ounce, earns $250 per ounce, or $250 million when gold is $400/oz. ($12.86/gg). If gold rises to $500/oz. ($16.08/gg), its earnings rise by $100 million, or 40 percent. Miner B's cost is $350/oz. ($11.25/gg), which means it earns only $50 million with gold at $400, but $150 million when gold goes to $500, a gain of 300 percent. Investors tend to reward percentage gains, so in this example, you'd expect miner B's stock to outperform. Unlike the hedging argument, we're not taking a firm stand on operating leverage. Whether the potential reward is worth the added risk is a matter for each investor to decide.

Currency leverage. Gold producers operate in different parts of the world, using different currencies. And their operating costs—labor, interest, and supplies—become more or less expensive when the value of the local currency changes. Consider a miner in, say, South Africa, which pays its workers in rands, the local currency. When the rand strengthens versus gold, the South African miner's costs go up in relation to the price it receives for its gold, thus lowering its profit.

For most of the 1990s, the rising dollar worked to foreign miners' advantage, lowering their costs in terms of the world's main currency. Now, however, the process is shifting into reverse. To understand what this means, say gold rises by 50 percent versus the dollar, but the rand, as the currency of a gold-producing country, appreciates by, say, 25 percent against the dollar. Gold has effectively gone up only 25 percent for South African miners, a pretty good gain, but only half the benefit derived by a U.S.-based miner, which gets the full 50 percent as gold soars in relation to the supplies it buys and wages it pays.

Gold leverage. A miner like Goldcorp, which not only doesn't hedge but accumulates gold in place of cash, is profoundly affected by changes in gold's exchange rate. That is, it has a high degree of gold leverage. An active hedger, on the other hand, has locked in its selling price and doesn't much care where gold trades in the near term. To take an extreme example, Australian miner Sons of Gwalia has sold forward not just next year's production but *its entire reserve base,* which has a life of perhaps seven years. So unless it discovers more gold, for the next seven years it's a gold-mining company in name only, with a revenue stream that has no connection to gold's future exchange rate.

Quality of management. When you buy shares in a gold producer, you're of course buying its reserves and all the other things that we've covered so far. But you're also buying a management team. And nothing, perhaps not even gold in the ground, is as important in the long run, because good management translates into wise decisions. For gold-mining companies, that means the efficient operation of existing mines, financing and exploration strategies with the right mix of caution and opportunism, and effective communication with shareholders and Wall Street. And it means the acquisition of more low-cost reserves at attractive prices, not a simple matter with virtually every other miner attempting the same thing. Yet some management teams are able to do these things consistently. The result is that their companies grow, and the income flowing to their investors rises faster than for the industry as a whole. You'll want to be on the same side as these guys.

How do you identify them? Start with their records. Past success is of course no guarantee of future results, but if a given management team has consistently enriched its investors, then it's reasonable to assume they'll keep it up. As it is for so many other positive things, Newmont is a good example of what we're talking about. Beginning in 1997, as gold's decline made reserves nice and cheap, Newmont began gobbling up other high-quality operators like Santa Fe Pacific Gold, Battle Mountain Gold, Normandy, and Franco-Nevada. By 2002 it was the world's largest gold producer, but—importantly—it had become so without overleveraging. Its debt, as this is written in early 2004, is less than one-fourth of its total capital, while its market cap is about three times its 2000 level.

Much of the credit for Newmont's recent success goes to president Pierre Lassonde, who joined the company from Franco-Nevada, which he helped build and then merge with Newmont in 2000. Based on his work at Franco-Nevada and his tenure at Newmont, Lassonde is generally considered to be one of the smartest, if not the smartest, executives in the mining business. It's safe to say that a good part of Newmont's current market value is due to investors betting on a continuation of Lassonde's proven record. To analyze the management teams of other miners, use the following criteria:

Experience. What have they done in the past that's relevant to gold mining? Engineering degrees, leadership positions in industry organizations, contacts in the financial world, are all helpful. But be aware that great miners don't necessarily make great CEOs. When someone ascends from one level to the next, view them with skepticism until they've proven themselves.

Longevity and stability. How long have they been at their present jobs? Obviously, a long, successful tenure is reassuring, and a lot of bouncing around is questionable.

Recent results. Have their decisions borne fruit? A rising stock price relative to their peers is probably the only thing that most people look at to assess a company's management, and in many cases it's enough.

Reasonable plans. Do their current plans seem reasonable based on your sense of the market and the strategies of other well-managed companies?

Good corporate governance. After the excesses of the 1990s, governance practices are, quite rightly, under the microscope. So consider the following:

- Are the committees that elect board members and set executive pay independent—that is, not beholden to management? They should be, to ensure their ability to attract people who will do more than just rubber-stamp management's decisions.

- Are executive pay packages consistent with the rest of the industry? Executives overpaying themselves is, as we've learned so painfully in the past few years, a huge red flag. Good managers make big bucks only when their shareholders do.

- Do insiders own a lot of stock? You're better off with companies in which the managers are also large shareholders (like Newmont, where at year-end 2003 Lassonde and several other executives owned 15 million shares). An executive who's also a major shareholder is risking his personal fortune alongside yours and will have the same goal as you—a higher stock price.

- Are auditors also consultants? The accountants going over a company's books should not be paid by the company for other work. That creates too many conflicts of interest.

Corporate governance is a still-evolving issue that's far too complicated to be fully covered here. But it matters, both because good governance produces good results and because Wall Street now believes that it does.

Acquirer or acquiree? Gold mining is always a beehive of mergers and acquisitions, but lately the pace has accelerated. Why? Mostly because of the gold investment community's relatively narrow focus. The media tends to mention the same handful of majors, and money managers own them in greater proportion than smaller players. As a result, the market places a higher value on the majors' reserves, which is another way of saying that capital is cheaper for majors than for less widely followed juniors and mid-tiers. Access to this cheap capital allows the majors to grow by buying up the reserves of smaller miners. Once incorporated into a major's portfolio, these reserves are valued by the market at the major's higher per-ounce market value. This makes such acquisitions "accretive," by adding more to earnings than they cost. So majors are able to let smaller companies do the risky exploration work, then swoop in and buy them up once their properties are demonstrably valuable. Bigger really is better, in other words, which explains the constant drumbeat of recent mergers among the majors. The table on page 125 lists a few of the recent highlights.

For investors there are three points of interest here:

- The majors' advantages are real and likely to stay real for a while, which gives them considerably better growth prospects than you might expect from leaders in a mature industry. This is especially true for the conservatively capitalized majors, which have massive borrowing ability should they choose to use it. So don't be surprised when one of the majors you bought because of its rock-solid balance sheet suddenly leverages itself to the hilt to make a huge acquisition. This kind of empire building happens in every bull market, as CEOs start focusing on their legacy rather than tending to the mundane particulars of day-to-day business. Your conservative portfolio can be transformed into something much more aggressive at the stroke of a CEO's pen. Be careful.

- As a smaller miner grows and its visibility increases, expect its market value to rise more quickly than its gold output. This is due to the growing number of people willing to buy in as its success draws media and investor attention. So a small company's ability to grow through acquisition is important. To judge this, begin with its finances. Does it already carry so much debt (whether in the form of bank loans or a gold hedge book) that taking on more will be a problem? Then its ability to buy other assets is limited. Or is it debt-free, which implies that it has plenty of available capital? And are there properties that make strategic sense? An Australian miner buying a South American mine might be stretching its management too thin, while a Canadian miner buying the property right next to its most productive mine creates a lot of synergy. Now we're getting into the real nuts and bolts of the mining business; to learn more, consider subscribing to one of the newsletters mentioned in Chapter 22 that focuses on topics like this.

RECENT GOLD-MINING MERGERS/ACQUISITIONS

Year	Buyer	Target	Deal value ($ millions)
1998	Ashanti	SAMAX	140
1998	Newmont	Santa Fe	2,500
1999	Homestake	Argentina Gold	200
1999	Placer Dome	South Deep	250
1999	Barrick	Sutton	620
1999	Placer Dome	Getchel	1,100
2000	Gold Fields	Damang	50
2000	AngloGold	Morila	170
2000	Barrick	Pangea	190
2000	AngloGold	Geita	300
2000	Newmont	Battle Mountain	600
2000	Franco-Nevada	Euro-Nevada	1,200
2001	Goldfields	Delta Gold	500
2001	Barrick	Homestake	2,300
2001	Goldfields	WMC Gold	520
2002	Placer Dome	AurionGold	790
2002	Newmont	Franco-Nevada and Normandy	4,350
2003	Placer Dome	EAGM	290
2003	Harmony	ARMGold	900
2003	AngloGold	Ashanti	1,130
2003	Kinross	Echo Bay and TVX	1,400

Source: Mineweb

- Juniors become takeover candidates to the extent that they're successful in turning speculative properties into real gold mines. As gold enters the wild stage of its current bull market, juniors might experience the kind of feeding frenzy that greeted tech-stock IPOs in the late 1990s.

BUILDING A PORTFOLIO OF GOLD-MINING STOCKS

Now, at last, we come to the fun part: building a portfolio of gold-mining stocks. To do this successfully, begin by looking in the mirror. To steal a great line from Adam Smith's classic *Money Game*, if you don't know who you are, the stock market is an expensive place to find out. And while we're as certain as we've ever been that the dollar and gold are going to part ways in the coming decade, nothing in life is guaranteed. There is risk involved in any investment, and mining stocks are among the most capricious of all. So think about how much volatility you can tolerate. Will you be able to sleep if your portfolio is temporarily down 20 percent? Are you prepared to kick out the losers to prevent your portfolio from dropping 40 percent? The greater your tolerance for risk, the more aggressive you can be in structuring a portfolio. Other questions to ask yourself include:

- What's your objective? Capital appreciation, capital preservation, dividend income, or some combination thereof?
- What's your time frame? If you'll need a given piece of capital in three years, you'll want a conservative stance regardless of your risk tolerance. If you won't be spending it for twenty years, then you can afford to bet on trends that might take a while to play out.
- How well do you understand investing? The more you know, the more decisions you can make yourself and the more risks you can take on.
- How much time do you have to devote to your investments? The less time, the more conservative you'll want to be.

Once you've painted your investing self-portrait, you're ready to structure a portfolio of mining stocks. We've named names here to illustrate various points, but because of the time that will elapse between this writing and whenever it is that you'll read this, *do not* view these sample portfolios as buy recommendations. They're meant as examples only, based on information available at the time of writing in early 2004.

SAMPLE PORTFOLIOS

Conservative. You want to build capital and generate income while preserving the purchasing power of your money and avoiding unpleasant surprises. That means owning mostly low-production-cost, diversified,

CONSERVATIVE PORTFOLIO		
Company	Ticker	Market Value 12/31/03 (US$ mill.)
Gold Fields	GFI	6,880
Goldcorp	GG	2,730
Newmont	NEM	17,637
IAMGOLD	IAG	955
Glamis	GLG	2,190

well-capitalized, dividend-paying majors, along with a few rock-solid mid-tiers. These stocks, because they're already known quantities and widely held by mutual funds, won't soar like the more speculative mid-tiers and juniors, but they will rise along with gold's exchange rate, and they'll do so without the volatility of their lesser competitors.

Balanced. You want to own at least a couple of the huge winners that gold's bull market will produce, without taking on unnecessary risk. So you mix and match, buying some of the more aggressive majors and stronger mid-tiers, along with maybe one or two promising juniors, just to make it interesting. These stocks will move more—both up and down—than gold, so your returns will be an exaggerated version of gold's trajectory. You'll earn somewhat more than with the conservative portfolio, at the cost of some extra thrills and chills along the way.

BALANCED PORTFOLIO		
Company	Ticker	Market Value 12/31/03 (US$ mill.)
Agnico-Eagle	AEM	1,110
Gold Fields	GFI	6,880
Goldcorp	GG	2,730
Harmony	HMY	3,241
Meridian	MDG	1,361
Newmont	NEM	17,637
Rio Narcea	RNG.TO	318
Royal Gold	RGLD	410

Aggressive. You're intrigued by our prediction of global financial chaos and a soaring gold exchange rate—and you can take risks and still sleep well—so you go for the big prize. Your portfolio consists of some of the more aggressive mid-tiers, along with the most promising juniors and property plays. Several of the property plays will fail for various reasons, costing you everything you put into them, and possibly causing your whole portfolio to fall temporarily. But several others will go up by multiples of their purchase price. You should do very well overall, and you'll certainly never be bored.

AGGRESSIVE PORTFOLIO

Company	Ticker	Market Value 12/31/03 (US$ mill.)
Crystallex (property play)	KRY	210
Durban Deep	DROOY	860
Freeport McMoran Copper & Gold	FCX	7,340
High River Gold	HRG.TO	150
Kinross Gold	KGC	2,640
Rio Narcea	RNG.TO	318
Royal Gold	RGLD	410

Chapter 15

PRECIOUS-METALS MUTUAL FUNDS

If your reaction to the previous chapter is that analyzing gold-mining stocks seems like a lot of work, don't worry. Few people have the time or inclination to create and monitor a portfolio of gold-mining or any other kind of stocks. Most would rather have someone else do it for them, which is why the mutual fund business is so huge.

Even in a relatively small niche like precious metals, there are plenty of funds to choose from. But they aren't identical, so do a little research to find the funds that best fit your personality and investment objectives. Look for the right mix of stocks, in terms of size, leverage, revenue policy, and geographic exposure. And seek out a fund manager who buys and sells in a way that makes you comfortable. You won't find a perfect fit, but with a little digging you can get close. Here are the main things to understand about the funds you consider:

Load/no load. Fees associated with buying or selling funds are known as "loads." In most cases, they simply reimburse the financial advisor who handles the paperwork and don't improve the performance of the fund, making load funds as a group a lot less interesting than their no-load competitors. The funds listed on page 132 are all no load, since, other things being equal, that's the place to start. There are, however, rare instances where paying a load is justified—if you work with a trusted financial planner and that's how he gets paid, for instance. And if a load fund is extraordinary in its focus or performance (Fidelity Magellan when it was run by the legendary Peter Lynch comes to mind), it may be worth the added cost.

Assets under management. Bigger funds tend to be more stable and better able to take large positions in really promising companies. But beyond a certain point, a large fund finds itself owning practically everything worth owning, tying its managers' hands and making their judgment a lot less important. So the ideal fund is big enough to be stable and small enough to be nimble. What that means in terms of assets will vary with the overall size of this market and the cash being directed toward it by investors.

Management tenure. A fund gets to keep its track record even when the people who gave it that record move on. So look not just at a fund's three- or five-year returns, but its results during the current manager's tenure. Luckily, the gold fund world is small, giving money managers few opportunities to job-hop. So most of the funds listed here have been run by the same people for a while, meaning that they have compiled the funds' records.

Expense ratio. At first glance, cost looks like the Achilles' heel of the gold fund community. With only a couple of exceptions, even the best-run no-load funds charge a significant amount of money for the privilege of investing in them. Of the funds listed here, management fees range from a reasonable .7 percent to over 3 percent, with an average of around 2 percent. That's high, but not totally without justification. Mining stocks are a specialized area, making it expensive to attract managers with expertise in mining and geology. Meanwhile, mining companies are located throughout the world, requiring fund managers to visit hard-to-reach places like Eritrea or Papua New Guinea.

Turnover. This is the measure of how frequently a fund manager buys and sells, expressed in an annual percentage. Turnover of 50 percent means that on average a fund replaces half the stocks in its portfolio in a given year: 100 percent means it replaces them all. A fund that holds its stocks for years would therefore have a much lower turnover than one that trades actively. We wouldn't sell any of the better precious-metals stocks at 2003 prices, so we're suspicious of high-turnover funds. Why would they waste the effort?

Focus. Like any other sector fund, precious-metals funds can take wildly varying approaches to their markets. Some own only majors, while some go for more obscure mid-tiers and speculative "property play" companies that may not even be producing at the moment. Some like hedgers, and some prefer unhedged miners. Some hold physical gold and/or derivatives along with their stocks. The most conservative end of the spectrum would be a large fund that holds mostly unhedged majors. Middle-of-the-road funds hold unhedged majors and mid-tiers, and so on, with the most aggressive funds holding mostly unhedged mid-tiers and juniors.

Open- or closed-end. The vast majority of precious-metals funds are "open-end," which means they can take in new money and invest it as they see fit. When the market closes, they total up the changes in their various holdings and compute a net asset value, or NAV. This is the price that you pay to invest in such a fund. Because the NAV can be computed only after the markets have closed, your purchase price is the NAV at the end of the day on which you invest.

"Closed-end" funds don't accept new investors. Instead, they are bought and sold like stocks during the course of the trading day. As a result, a closed-end fund might trade above or below its NAV, depending on market sentiment. All the funds in the table on page 132 are open-end except the Central Fund of Canada, which, besides being closed-end, holds gold and silver bullion instead of mining shares. It's an easy, interesting way to buy these precious metals. But recently, because

NO-LOAD PRECIOUS-METALS MUTUAL FUNDS

Fund	Symbol	Assets $ mill.*	Expense ratio %	Tenure of current manager	Turnover %	% of assets North America	% of assets South Africa
American Century Global Gold	BGEIX	552	0.7	11 years	37	64	18
Central Fund of Canada†	CEF	132	0.9	20 years	NA	100‡	0
Gabelli Gold	GOLDX	249	2.9	9 years	37	62	25
Invesco Gold & Precious Metals	FGLDX	138	2.3	4 years	60	80	4
Rydex Precious Metals	RYPMX	106	1.3	3 years	150	75	15
Tocqueville Gold	TGLDX	232	1.6	5 years	28	75	14
US Global Gold	USERX	66	3.5	NA	120	60	12
US Global World Precious Metals	UNWPX	170	2.2	NA	41	70	10
USAA Gold	USAGX	240	1.5	9 years	22	80	7

* As of 9/30/03
† Closed-end fund
‡ Owns primarily gold bullion

Source: Fund statements, Eaglewing Guide to Gold Funds

of the growing interest in gold, Central Fund has been trading at a premium to the value of its holdings. At the end of 2003, this premium was about 9 percent, meaning that new investors were paying a little over $430 an ounce when gold was at $400. So keep an eye on it, and if the premium drops to a reasonable level (or goes negative, as sometimes happens with closed-end funds), give this fund serious consideration.

Be sure to diversify. Funds, like stocks, can have ups and downs that are unrelated to their market. The recent "fund-timing" scandals, for instance, illustrate how even seemingly rock-solid money managers can succumb to temptation, hurting their investors in ways that have nothing to do with the level of the Dow or the price of gold. And even the best money managers make bad decisions. So no matter how perfect a given fund seems, don't give it more than half of your capital. Buy two or perhaps three, even if the others are less attractive, and then monitor and adjust your portfolio as your needs and the markets change.

PHYSICAL OR PAPER GOLD: WHICH IS THE BETTER DEAL?

On December 8, 2003, *Barron's* magazine rocked the gold market with an article claiming that gold-mining stocks, which had soared in recent months, were overvalued in relation to their gold reserves. And sure enough, whether because the analysis was on point or because *Barron's* is influential, gold's exchange rate rose modestly in the ensuing couple of weeks while gold stocks got hammered.

This episode illustrates one of the central challenges facing anyone who is building a gold-based portfolio: how to tell which of the many possibilities is the best deal, relatively speaking. Are one-ounce bars cheap relative to mining stocks, or vice versa? And how big (and therefore compelling) is the value gap? Excellent questions. Here's how to answer them: For an individual mining stock, go through the analytical steps outlined in Chapter 14, and compare the result to gold's exchange rate, both current and expected. Then take the markup on gold bullion

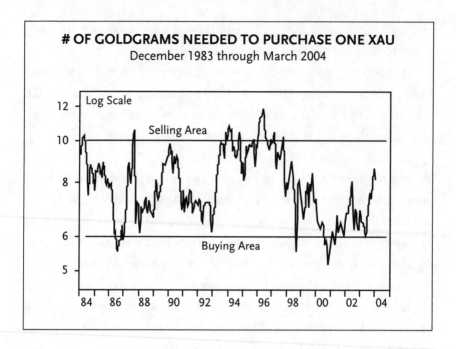

OF GOLDGRAMS NEEDED TO PURCHASE ONE XAU
December 1983 through March 2004

into account, and you'll have a good idea of whether bullion or stock is more attractive at the moment.

To compare physical gold to gold-mining shares in general, compare gold's exchange rate to a good index of mining shares, like the XAU, which contains most of the major gold producers. As you can see from the chart above, based on recent history, when it takes 10gg or more to purchase one unit of the XAU, mining stocks are expensive compared to bullion and likely to underperform in the coming year. Conversely, when it takes 6gg or less to purchase one XAU, mining stocks are relatively cheap. (Current goldgram exchange rates for the dollar and other major currencies are available at www.goldmoney.com.) Though the XAU rose strongly in the first three years of this decade, by the end of 2003, it was still within the "cheap" part of its historical range. Our conclusion: *Barron's* was jumping the gun a bit. But that's to be expected in bull markets; along the way you'll read lots of negative opinion based on solid-sounding analysis. Don't let it shake your conviction.

Chapter 16

OTHER PRECIOUS METALS

G old is the dominant precious metal, but it isn't the only one. There are others, each unique in its own way, but all likely to benefit from a collapsing dollar. Here are some of them:

SILVER: GOOD AS GOLD?

For most of human history, silver has been right there beside gold, sometimes competing, other times complementing, but almost always seen as another genuine form of money. So will the dramatic events that return gold to the center of the monetary world affect silver as well? Yes indeed. Silver's future is a little different from gold's, but in many ways—as a store of value and profitable investment—just as bright. So let's begin this story at the point where gold and silver parted ways.

After the U.S. government confiscated its citizens' gold in 1933, silver coins continued to circulate as the dimes, quarters, half-dollars, and silver dollars that many of us remember from our childhood. But as government spending soared in the late 1960s, so did the supply of paper dollars. Silver held its value while dollars were losing theirs, and the silver in a given coin came to be worth more than the face value of the coin itself. Americans, adhering to Gresham's Law, began hoarding silver and spending paper, with the result that silver coins dropped out of circulation. Bad money drove out good. These days, the silver in 1960s-era coins is worth about five times the face value of the coins themselves, so while they're still legal tender, for the most part they now reside next to their gold cousins in coin collections and safe-deposit boxes.

But where gold demand has remained mostly monetary—that is, new production is bought up by people wanting to store wealth, whether in the form of coins, bars, or high-karat jewelry—silver in the twentieth century became an industrial commodity, with a price (note that since silver is no longer money, we refer to its price rather than its exchange rate) that depends on demand from users rather than collectors or investors. Here's a brief overview of its markets.

Photography. Today's photographic film is based on the insights of an Englishman named William Talbot, who in the 1830s discovered that silver halides, which form when silver reacts with "halogens" like iodine, chlorine, and bromine, were extraordinarily light-sensitive. The color film in your camera is a direct though more sophisticated descendant of Talbot's earliest concoctions, with three "emulsion layers" of tiny silver bromide crystals in a gelatin glue, each sensitive to red, green, or blue light. When struck by light, the crystals reconfigure, producing a rectangle of "exposed" film that can be developed into a color print. The development process involves immersing the exposed film in a solution that strips off the silver, allowing it to be recovered and recycled.

Silverware and Jewelry. Silver is shiny, harder than gold, and much cheaper, so it has been popular since the dawn of recorded history for adornment and, for the last few centuries, as high-status tableware. This category accounts for nearly a third of silver demand.

Electronics and Industrial. Silver's high electrical and thermal conductivity, malleability, and corrosion resistance make it one of modern technology's favorite materials. On/off switches used in electrical equipment and

2002 SILVER DEMAND

Sector	Annual demand (mill./oz.)	Percent of total
Electronics and Batteries	342.4	40
Jewelry and Silverware	259.2	30
Photography	205.3	24
Coins	31.3	4
Other	24.8	2
Total	863.0	100

Source: Silver Institute

appliances work best with silver. The metal is also used as a solder to bond metal surfaces, as a biocide to keep microbial infestations at bay, and as a transparent coating for thermal windows. It's a crucial part of most solar panels and of superconducting wire, which conducts electricity with little or no resistance (and might just revolutionize the power business in the coming decade). According to the Silver Institute, a mile of state-of-the-art superconducting wire contains about 1,000 ounces of silver.

Coins and Bars. As with gold, the world's governments have noticed a growing interest in silver as a store of value and are once again minting silver coins. This part of the silver market is relatively tiny, but it's growing quickly as people seek sound money alternatives to fiat currencies.

The silver deficit. Now, here's where silver's story becomes really interesting. In an average year, a little over 800 million ounces of silver are consumed by its various users. But less than 600 million ounces are produced by mines around the world. This shortfall is met in two ways: Silver-laden photographic film and silver from many industrial uses is recycled, allowing some silver to be used over and over again. But more important, aboveground stocks of silver are being drawn down, as central banks and other big holders of silver sell off their stockpiles. The result is that the world's silver inventory has been shrinking steadily. The U.S. government, which had more than six billion ounces of silver in the 1940s, now has none. China's official silver holdings fell by more than 50 million ounces in 2002 alone and will, at the present rate of decline, be eliminated within a couple of years. And inventories at Comex, the world's major silver-trading exchange, fell from 330 million ounces in 1980 to about 100 million in 2003. Overall, the available stockpile of silver has declined from more than 2.5 billion ounces in 1980 to around 500 million ounces today, or less than is used in a single year.

And unlike gold, most of which is still around, a good portion of each year's silver production is consumed and lost forever. In electronics especially, the amount of silver used in a given component is often so small that it's not worth recycling. Your computer keyboard, for instance, contains less than a quarter's worth of silver, making it economically impractical to retrieve when you toss it in the trash.

Viewed this way, silver is a great commodity play, i.e., something that will spike in price simply because of an imbalance between supply and demand, even if the economy keeps growing steadily—in fact,

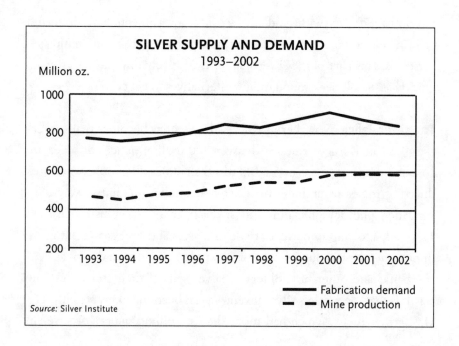

SILVER SUPPLY AND DEMAND
1993–2002

Million oz.

Source: Silver Institute

Fabrication demand
Mine production

especially if it does. In other words, it won't take a monetary crisis to produce a bull market in silver. Market forces will cause a shortage, which, other things being equal, will cause its price to rise.

Dig a little deeper, and the story gets even better. It seems that the most commonly cited "flaws" in the bullish case for silver are fallacies. Consider:

Digital photography will cause demand for silver to collapse. Anyone who has used both a traditional 35mm camera and a new digital camera knows that digital is vastly better. Clearly, the days of 35mm photography for the mass consumer market are numbered, and you'd expect the demise of film to be a huge negative for silver. This prospect really began weighing on the silver market in 2003, when Kodak, the biggest U.S. maker of photographic film, announced that it was abandoning its work on new films and would thereafter focus on the digital side of its business.

Does this mean the end of silver in the photography business? Not at all. First, we're viewing this process through affluent Western eyes. In most of the world, paying $200 for a digital camera is still a fantasy. So relatively cheap, silver-consuming snapshot cameras will see growing demand for years to come. Kodak, for its part, will continue to sell a lot of film, even if its future lies elsewhere. Second, and vastly more important, photographic film is not just a source of demand for silver but also a source of supply. Recall that recycled silver is one of the major ways that we fill the silver deficit. One study estimates that nearly 90 percent of the silver used in color photography is recycled. So less film usage means less recycled silver, a decrease in supply that nearly offsets the drop in demand. In any event, digital photography still requires silver. To accommodate the growing demand for digital print photo finishing, regional photo labs and minilabs are installing equipment that prints on silver-halide paper. The upshot: Even if the photography world goes totally digital tomorrow, the silver deficit will remain.

Rising silver prices will lead to rising mine output. With wheat, oil, or most any other commodity, higher prices do indeed lead to higher output, which eventually sends prices back to where they started. But that won't happen with silver, because most mined silver is a by-product of mining other minerals. And silver is generally such a small part of the mining cost equation that a rising silver price won't cause, say, a zinc mine to expand its production. Meanwhile, there are very few major silver mines in operation, and it takes years to bring new ones online, so silver's price can soar without causing a huge burst of new mine output. Economists call this "inelasticity of supply," meaning that a rising price doesn't automatically lead to rising supply.

Silver demand will fall if prices rise. If silver's price soars, we'll buy less of it, right? Wrong again. Silver is such a small part of the cost of most things it goes into that its price is almost irrelevant. Consider a pair of diamond-stud silver earrings. The diamonds might cost several hundred to several thousand dollars. The jeweler's labor and design creativity might run nearly as much, depending on the complexity of the work. But, assuming the silver content is half an ounce (which would still make for some very big earrings), the silver might cost $3 at late-2003 prices. Let silver go to $25 an ounce, and its share of the earrings' cost goes to $12.50, still negligible in the scheme of things. The story is the same in electronics, where the thin silver films that allow printed circuits to perform their miracles amount to tiny fractions of an ounce per chip or switch. So with the relatively minor exception of silver cutlery, a rising silver price will hardly affect demand at all.

The world's governments will keep dumping silver, just as they do gold, depressing its price forever. They might if they could, but as we noted above, they can't. The U.S. government is tapped out and now must buy silver on the open market in order to mint new Silver Eagles. China is heading that way fast, and no other central bank has enough silver to make a difference. Add it all up and you get a continuing (though perhaps somewhat smaller) imbalance between supply and demand, and dwindling aboveground stocks available to satisfy the deficit.

Now let's look at some silver facts that are *not* fallacies:

The silver market is tiny. One way to gauge how far a commodity's price can move is to compare the size of its market to the pool of available capital. That is, if there's only a little of something, and a load of capital set to start chasing it, you have the potential for massive price increases. So for silver to rise dramatically, it would be helpful if its supply was small in relation to global money flows. Is it? No. "Small" really doesn't do it justice. Minuscule or microscopic would be a lot more appropriate.

In an average year, as we noted earlier, about 600 million ounces of silver are mined. At the $6-per-ounce price that prevailed at the end of 2003, this new supply was worth about $3.6 billion. The available aboveground stocks of silver totaled about 500 million ounces, worth about $3 billion. Compare this $6.6 billion total with the other markets listed below, and it's clear that a tiny fraction of these resources, if redirected to the silver market, would cause its price to soar.

It's cheap compared to stocks. The Dow/silver ratio bottomed in 1980 at 18:1, which means that it took 18 ounces of silver to buy one share of the Dow Jones Industrial Average. Then stocks and silver parted ways,

SILVER IN THE SCHEME OF THINGS

Market	Value at year-end 2003 ($ billions)
Available silver stockpiles plus annual mine production (at $6/oz.)	7
Annual global gold production (80 million ounces at $400/oz.)	32
Microsoft's cash on hand	50
Market value of all publicly traded gold-mining companies	100
Microsoft's market value	275
Combined assets of Fannie Mae and Freddie Mac	1,700
Annual U.S. government spending	2,300
Value of all California single-family homes (12 million homes with an average value of $300,000 each)	3,600
U.S. GDP	10,500
Global GDP	32,000
Total U.S. debt	37,000
Notional value of all global derivatives	200,000

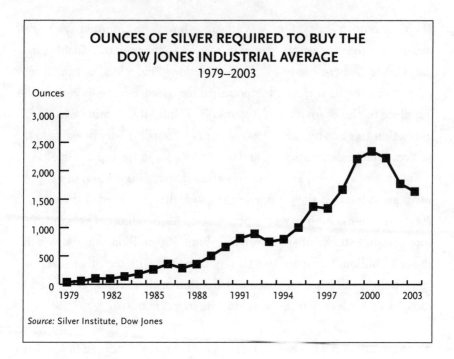

**OUNCES OF SILVER REQUIRED TO BUY THE
DOW JONES INDUSTRIAL AVERAGE**
1979–2003

Ounces

Source: Silver Institute, Dow Jones

and by 2000, it took nearly 2,500 ounces of silver to buy the Dow. By the end of 2003, the ratio stood at 1,636, a little below its peak but far, far above both its 1979 trough and its historical average.

It's cheap compared to real estate. The average family's home has been its best investment over the past few years, so it makes sense to include real estate in any list of competing assets. How does silver stack up to home prices? You can guess the answer. According to the Department of Housing and Urban Development, in 1979 it took 3,000 ounces of silver to buy the average new U.S. house. By the end of 2003, it took a whopping 33,000 ounces.

It's cheap compared to gold. Back when they both circulated as currencies, gold and silver were generally exchanged at a fixed ratio, usually in the range of 15:1 in favor of gold. That is, fifteen ounces of silver would exchange for one ounce of gold. In 1980, the gold/silver ratio was

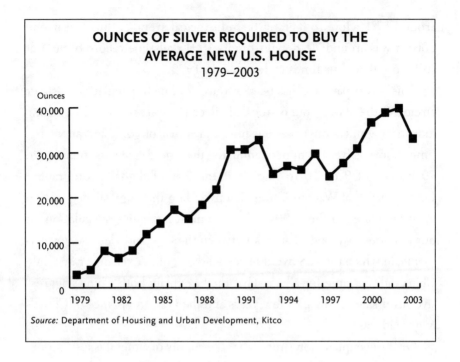

OUNCES OF SILVER REQUIRED TO BUY THE AVERAGE NEW U.S. HOUSE
1979–2003

Source: Department of Housing and Urban Development, Kitco

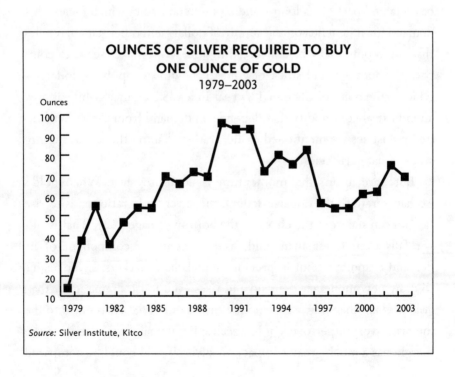

OUNCES OF SILVER REQUIRED TO BUY ONE OUNCE OF GOLD
1979–2003

Source: Silver Institute, Kitco

around 17:1, close to its long-term historical average. But at year-end 2003 it was around 70, down from its 1991's all-time record of 96, but still more than four times higher than in 1979.

This "silver paradox" has been a source of much speculation in silver circles: If the aboveground stock of silver (in warehouses and existing industrial applications) is about nine times that of gold, and about ten times more silver is mined annually than gold, why is their ratio 70 instead of 9 or 10 to one? Is it the fear of digital photography? Or concern that Warren Buffett is unwinding the huge silver position he accumulated in the 1990s? Or—the most intriguing speculation, in our opinion—was a deal struck between the U.S. and Chinese governments, in which the U.S. would keep a lid on gold's exchange rate while China did the same for silver? That might explain both China's aggressive silver sales of the past few years and the U.S. acceptance of China's huge trade surplus.

Or is the explanation simply that the supply of a metal is less important than demand in determining its value? Gold, despite all it travails, has retained part of its long-standing monetary role, which means that demand for it depends on the supply of dollars and other fiat currencies that could potentially be converted to gold. So it makes sense to compare the aboveground stock of gold to the global supply of dollars— which is the point of Chapter 11's Fear Index. Silver, meanwhile, is now an industrial commodity that depends on demand from the rather limited industries we mentioned earlier, rather than on the world's entire stock of fiat currencies.

But here again, the momentum is about to shift. When gold's exchange rate to the dollar is falling, the silver/gold ratio tends to rise (as you can see from the chart on the bottom of page 143). That is, silver falls even faster than gold, as the monetary component of its demand evaporates. But in precious-metals bull markets, silver begins to draw new monetary demand and rises even more dramatically than gold. Put another way, when money rushes out of fiat currency into the metals, silver outperforms gold because the demand for metals on the margin has a much greater impact on silver. If gold could be compared to a Boeing 747, then silver is an F-16. An F-16 takes off on a dime and is pointing toward the stratosphere in moments, while a 747 takes (relatively speaking) ages to gain altitude.

Will this pattern hold in the coming decade? Almost certainly, and the results will be spectacular. Say, for example, that gold rises to $1,000 (which it will within a very short time) and that the silver/gold ratio falls to a still-quite-high thirty. That means thirty ounces of silver will buy one ounce of gold, implying a silver price of $33. With gold starting at $400 and silver at $6, the result is that gold's exchange rate increases by 150 percent, while silver soars 450 percent.

How to own silver. If you've read Chapters 13 and 14, you already know, generally, how to prepare for silver's bull market, since the process is very similar to buying gold. The numbers are just a lot smaller.

Bullion coins. Many countries mint silver bullion coins, some of the more popular of which are listed below. Silver can also be bought in bags of pre-1965 "Investment Grade Silver Bullion" dimes, quarters, and half-dollars. Generally, they're worn to the point that $1,000 of face value equals a little over 700 ounces. Other than that, approach silver bullion as you would gold: Choose your dealer carefully, get the best deal on the right mix of coins, and store them safely. And, as with gold, to get the most silver for your money, buy larger bars, which are usually cheaper to make than coins.

Popular Silver Coins and Bars	US$ Price at 1/21/04
U.S. Silver Eagle, 1 oz.	8.85
Canadian Silver Maple Leaf, 1 oz.	8.47
Silver bar, 100 oz.	692
Silver bar, 1,000 oz.	6,520
Silver spot price/oz.	**6.19**

Source: Kitco

PUBLICLY TRADED SILVER-MINING COMPANIES

Company	Ticker	Market value 12/31/03 ($ millions)
Apex Silver*	SIL	827
Coeur d'Alene	CDE	1,308
Hecla Mining	HL	897
Pan American Silver	PAAS	796
Silver Standard Resources*	SSRI	480

* Property plays
Source: Yahoo! Finance

Silver-mining stocks. There are only a handful of pure silver-mining stocks out there. A rising silver price should do wonders for both their bottom lines and their market caps.

Mutual funds. Not a single mutual fund specializes in silver, but several precious-metals funds own decent amounts of silver stocks, and the previously mentioned Central Fund owns gold and silver bullion in a fixed ratio between the two. So go back to the list of funds in Chapter 15, and look at their top twenty-five holdings (available at fund-tracker Morningstar's Web site or in each fund's prospectus). If silver miners are well represented in a fund's portfolio, then it offers some exposure to this market.

PLATINUM AND PALLADIUM: THE OTHER PRECIOUS METALS

Platinum and palladium have never functioned as money and probably won't in the foreseeable future. But as the world's other two precious metals—and highly sought-after industrial commodities—they're nearly as likely as silver to be swept up in the coming hard-asset tidal wave. So you should understand them, both as alternatives for diversifying within precious metals and as commodity plays in their own right.

Platinum and palladium, along with rhodium, ruthenium, iridium, and osmium, are members of the platinum group of metals (PGMs).

They're also, along with gold and silver, "noble" metals, because of their high resistance to oxidation and corrosion. Sometimes called "white gold," platinum is the rarest of all the precious metals. Annual mine production is about 5.9 million ounces, or less than 6 percent of annual gold production and 1 percent of silver's. Eighty percent of the world's platinum comes from South Africa and 12 percent from Russia, with the rest dribbling in from a few mines in North and South America.

Like silver, platinum is an industrial commodity that is used rather than hoarded, but unlike silver only a small amount of it is recycled, so any production shortfall has to be met from aboveground stocks. The largest platinum stockpiles are held by the U.S., South African, and Russian governments, though Russian reports are considered by some to be unreliable. Both the U.S. and Russia have been selling off their stockpiles, and by the end of 2002 it was estimated that remaining inventories equaled only about two years of current consumption. Platinum's price is therefore extremely sensitive to changes in demand.

About 40 percent of each year's platinum production goes to the jewelry industry, where, because its rich white color enhances the sparkle of diamonds, it is rapidly displacing gold and silver as the setting of choice. Another 35 percent is used in automobile catalytic converters, devices that turn the toxic gases produced by unleaded gasoline into carbon dioxide and water. The rest flows to a wide range of industrial niches. Because it doesn't corrode, platinum is used by the chemical industry to make vats for the manufacture of acids. When mixed with cobalt, platinum can store tremendous amounts of information, making it the preferred medium for computer hard drives. It inhibits the growth of cancer cells, making it one of the main components of chemotherapy compounds. By one estimate, 20 percent of all the goods manufactured today either contain platinum or are produced using platinum-containing equipment.

Palladium is platinum's main competition in catalytic converters. More effective on diesel fuel engines, it is seeing strong demand as relatively clean diesel vehicles become more popular in Europe and Japan. The auto industry is researching ways to make palladium-based catalytic converters work well on gasoline engines, though so far the process hasn't yielded marketable results. Russia typically supplies about two-thirds of the world's palladium (mostly as a by-product of its platinum mining), and supply and demand are roughly in balance at about 5.5 million ounces each year.

Looking ahead, both metals have three big things going for them. First, they're important components of fuel cells, which generate electricity by breaking hydrogen into its constituent parts, and are increasingly seen as the successor technology to both internal combustion engines and fossil-fuel power plants. Second, like so many other things, platinum and palladium are "China plays." As more newly middle-class Chinese buy cars, and Chinese air pollution laws become more stringent, the demand for catalytic converters is rising. The same holds for India, which is growing nearly as fast as China and will, if current trends hold, become the world's most populous country by midcentury. Third, and most on-point for our purposes, investment demand for platinum and palladium coins is likely to ride the coattails of gold and silver. As

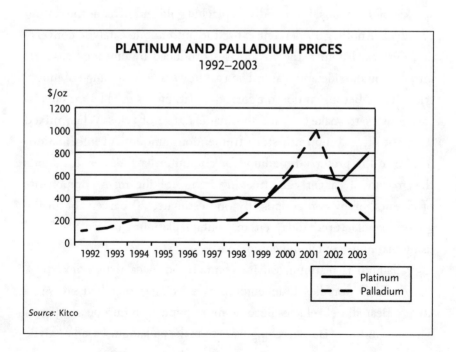

PLATINUM AND PALLADIUM PRICES
1992–2003

Source: Kitco

you'll see below, it's possible to buy coins made of these metals from the same dealers who sell gold and silver Eagles. Because the supply/demand situation is so precarious for both metals, a surge in demand from any of these three sources, let alone all three, would send their prices through the roof.

On the downside, since both platinum and palladium compete for many of the same industrial uses (while platinum competes with gold and silver in jewelry), demand for each is price-sensitive. So a surge by one might cause users to switch to other precious/noble metals, limiting or reversing the initial momentum. The power of this kind of "elasticity" was evident in 2001, when a spike in palladium's price caused a decline in demand, which in turn caused the price to retrace its steps and then some. And because these are industrial rather than monetary metals, demand for them falls when the economy slows.

Profiting from a noble-metals bull market. Assuming that at least one of the above sources of new demand—fuel cells, Chinese and Indian growth, or coin sales—materializes, these small, thin, precariously balanced markets could soar in coming years. And if you've read the chapters on gold coins and mining shares, you have a general idea how to profit from the trend. Platinum and palladium are mined by a handful of companies, the largest of which appear in the table below. Some of these stocks are thinly traded on U.S. markets, making them very illiquid and

PLATINUM/PALLADIUM MINERS

Company	Symbol	Headquarters	Market Cap 12/31/03 ($ mill.)
Anglo Platinum	AAPTF.PK	South Africa	NA
Aquarius Platinum	AQPBF.PK	South Africa	NA
Impala Platinum	IMPAF.PK	South Africa	NA
Lonmin	LNMIF.PK	South Africa	NA
Norilsk Nickel	NILSF.PK	Russia	NA
North American Palladium	PAL	Canada	428
Stillwater Mining	SWC	U.S.	884

hence risky. Others are primarily miners of nickel and other metals, making them less-than-pure noble-metal plays. So be careful, do some serious research, consult your broker, and after buying in, pay close attention.

Platinum and palladium bullion is available from the same dealers who carry gold and silver, though the selection is considerably less broad. Platinum Eagle coins come in sizes ranging from $1/10$ ounce to one ounce, while palladium is primarily available in one-ounce bars. Because these are low-volume items, they tend to have higher markups than gold and silver coins. And they're not as recognizable as gold and silver, making them considerably harder to sell. But in a global inflationary boom they might do very well nonetheless.

For more background and up-to-date information, visit the following Web sites:

www.infomine.com/commodities/platinum.asp
www.infomine.com/commodities/palladium.asp
www.platinum.matthey.com
www.platinuminfo.net

RARE COINS

Mention gold or silver coins to most people, and they immediately think of the Double Eagle gold piece or Liberty quarter that Grandpa gave them for their tenth birthday, which now resides in a dusty childhood coin collection last examined decades ago. Those coins aren't bullion. They're "numismatics," which, because of their age or rarity or both, tend to appeal to collectors rather than savers and are probably worth far more than their metal content. Numismatics are thus only tangentially related to trends in precious-metals prices and aren't one of the main ways to use gold or silver to protect your purchasing power.

That's not to say that rare coins are bad investments. On the contrary, many have been huge winners over the past couple of decades, and well-chosen numismatics will be double winners in a dollar collapse, benefiting from all the capital flowing into hard assets and the rising profile of precious metals in general. Another attraction of rare coins—and it's potentially a big one—is that if the government decides, once again, to confiscate gold bullion, coins dated prior to 1933 might not be included in the recall. For more details, two good sources are "Gold Confiscation: It could happen again" (Blanchard, 866-550-9093) and "How You Can Survive a Potential Gold Confiscation" (Centennial Precious Metals, 800-869-5115). Both reports conclude that governments, even those that prohibit gold ownership, are loath to confiscate rare coins, since these are more like Van Goghs than currency and are therefore not a threat to government power. Even totalitarian states like the Soviet Union permitted citizens to own rare coins. In the U.S., meanwhile, the exemption of numismatics from regulation has a long history, beginning with the original 1933 confiscation and running through Treasury regulations issued in the 1950s and 1960s. As you'll see presently, a whole category of coins is bought largely because of this protection.

So by all means hold on to that coin collection, and, if you're one of the rare breed with the time and inclination to really get to know this market, add to your holdings. Just don't make the mistake of thinking of numismatics as primarily gold and silver. They aren't and can rise and fall for a whole range of reasons unrelated to what we're predicting in this book. Some very good—and very long—books have been written on the intricacies of rare coins, and you'll want to read at least one of them before you start buying. In the meantime, here's an overview of the main traits that determine value in this market:

Condition. Collectors grade coin condition on a numerical scale running from 1 to 70. At the low end are "About Good," "Good," and "Very Good," which are mostly what you'll find in your childhood coin collection, if you still have it. As one industry source describes a "Good" coin, it is "Heavily worn with design visible but faint in areas. Many details are flat." "Very Good" coins are in a little better shape, but not good enough to interest collectors. As a result, coins in this range tend to behave more like bullion than Picassos.

The "investment grade" part of the spectrum begins at 50 and runs from "About Uncirculated" to "Mint," to "Proof." The first, as the name implies, describes a coin that hasn't been handled much, if at all. Mint coins were originally meant for circulation but, for whatever reason, weren't released, so they remain in pristine condition. Proof coins were never meant for circulation. They were specially struck on highly polished plates and have been handled with loving care ever since. Collectors care deeply about these distinctions. As you can see from the table below, a difference of ten points—which most people would hardly be able to detect—can be worth tens of thousands of dollars to collectors, since the rarity of the coin increases along with the grade.

Back in coin collecting's wild early days (pre-1980), the dealer who sold you a coin might also grade it—an obvious conflict of interest that made collecting a lot more risky. In response, the industry has turned to independent coin-grading firms like Professional Coin Grading Service (PCGS) and Numismatic Guaranty Corporation (NGC). These firms encase newly graded coins in a tamper-resistant plastic holder, with grade and certification number permanently displayed. PCGS and NGC also track the number of coins they see in each category, assigning "population" stats like 18/2, which means they've graded eighteen similar

U.S. INDIAN PRINCESS $3 GOLD PIECE
$ value at December 31, 2003

Date				Grade				
	AU	60	61	62	63	64	65	66
1859	1,100	2,475	2,875	4,050	6,825	9,425	27,000	—
1860	1,300	2,750	3,000	3,725	6,500	9,425	—	—
1861	1,575	3,525	3,775	4,550	7,800	13,500	—	—
1862	1,575	3,525	3,775	4,550	8,125	15,600	—	—
1863	1,575	3,525	3,775	4,825	8,125	13,700	23,500	32,000
1864	1,575	3,400	3,650	4,550	9,425	14,900	36,000	—
1865	5,525	10,000	11,400	14,300	21,000	34,000	46,000	—
1866	1,900	3,525	3,775	4,550	10,100	15,000	26,000	—
1867	2,100	3,525	3,775	6,325	9,100	14,200	28,000	—

Source: Professional Coin Grading Service

coins and found only two in better condition. The lower these numbers, the more attractive a coin is to collectors (with 1/0, of course, being the holy grail). With legitimacy of grade no longer an issue, thousands of coins are sold sight unseen each year, with relatively few complaints.

Rarity. Obviously, the fewer copies of a given coin that exist, the greater the worth of each coin. So the starting point in figuring out a coin's value is the number minted in the first place. There were just 528,000 St. Gaudens $20 gold pieces minted in 1921, for instance, and 4 million each year between 1922 and 1924. As the table below shows, this makes quite a difference in value today. And the 1933 St. Gaudens is perhaps the rarest coin of all. The Treasury hadn't released them when FDR banned gold ownership, so the Mint simply melted down the whole issue—except for five that found their way out the door. Four were eventually tracked down, and when the fifth showed up in 2002, it was (after some legal wrangling with Washington) auctioned off for a world-record rare-coin price of $7.5 million. Not a bad markup from $20.

To find the next batch of big winners, you'll need two things: unbiased information and a trustworthy dealer. Most coin aficionados turn to sources like the *RedBook,* an annual listing of the market price of virtually

U.S. ST. GAUDENS $20 GOLD PIECE
$ value at December 31, 2003

Date	Grade							
	60	**61**	**62**	**63**	**64**	**65**	**66**	**67**
1921	38,000	41,000	58,000	97,500	170,000	—	—	—
1922	525	570	585	650	865	4,750	—	—
1922-S*	900	1,000	1,150	2,300	6,000	41,000	—	—
1923	525	570	585	650	725	7,000	—	—
1923-D	525	570	585	650	900	1,500	3,600	11,000
1924	525	570	585	650	775	1,375	2,950	11,000
1924-D	1,950	2,275	3,000	6,000	11,000	—	—	—
1924-S	2,375	2,650	3,000	6,100	14,500	—		

* S and D refer to San Francisco and Denver, the cities where the coins were minted.
Source: Professional Coin Grading Service

every major coin, or the Web sites of PCGS and NGC, which offer background material and continuously updated pricing information. Choosing a dealer is a little trickier. There are many more rare-coin dealers than bullion dealers, so it's possible that a glance at the Yellow Pages will turn up several within a short drive. But don't just choose the closest one. Before giving them your money, find out a little about them, including:

- How much does the dealer know about the area that you'd like to specialize in? Some dealers specialize in sectors that might be unrelated to rare U.S. gold coins.
- What are their credentials within the numismatic community? Membership in the Professional Numismatist Guild (PNG), the only major numismatic organization that doesn't admit everyone who applies, is a big plus.
- How long have they been at it? Stability is a sign that they're following good business practices and satisfying their customers.
- Do they attend coin shows and auctions? This is the best way to stay current with the tastes of collectors and other dealers.
- Do they offer after-sale service? You'll want a teacher and sounding board, so accessibility and enthusiasm are crucial.

Talking to a good rare-coin dealer is a lot like talking to a stockbroker. They'll paint a picture of emerging trends and building collector interest, and push the coins that seem to be in the path of this momentum. If they're good, more often than not they'll be right, and some of the coins they recommend will generate good returns. But make no mistake: We're talking about the right coins bought for the right price and held long enough for their price to go up. Numismatics are anything but simple and never a sure thing.

And now a word about markups. With bullion, you know the underlying value of the coin's metal content and can easily calculate the premium you're paying. Not so with numismatics, where the markup is whatever the market will bear. So always research the price of a coin using third-party sources before buying, and understand that the bid/

ask spreads in this market will be higher than for bullion, and far higher than for stocks.

SEMI-NUMISMATICS

What if you like the idea of a little insurance against confiscation but have no desire to put in the effort—and pay the premiums over the gold content—to become a collector? Consider the "common" category of pre-1933 coins. These, as we mentioned, might be exempt from confiscation, but because there are a lot of them, they trade with a relatively small premium over their gold content—"bullion on steroids," as some dealers refer to them. The most popular of these "semi-rare" coins is the St. Gaudens $20 piece, which was minted in large numbers in the decades leading up to the Depression. As you saw in the table on page 153, the most common dates for these coins are available in nearly uncirculated condition for about 30 percent over the value of their gold content, with the premium shrinking even further as the condition dips into the "Good" range. These coins won't appreciate due to rarity, but will trade in line with gold prices, generally keeping whatever premium they had when you bought them. In other words, you'll pay $50–$100 more per ounce of gold, in return for which you get a little insurance against confiscation. And it's very possible that as we traverse the slippery slope of monetary crisis, the insurance feature will become more valuable, causing these coins to outperform their bullion cousins.

Is this insurance premium worth it? We're not sure. Being able to legally hold on to your gold when the government is confiscating bullion would be a nice option. On the other hand, these coins offer less gold for your money, when owning as much gold as possible should be your main goal. And numismatic coins' exemption from confiscation could in theory be eliminated if their growing popularity brings them to the attention of the anti-gold forces in future governments. In short, this is an issue without simple answers, where concepts like diversification are more important than estimates of relative return.

Chapter 17

STOCKS, BONDS, AND REAL ESTATE:

HOW OTHER ASSETS WILL FARE IN A CURRENCY CRISIS

With the dollar plunging on one hand and gold surging on the other, a lot of other asset classes will be no doubt be caught in the crossfire. How, for instance, does real estate hold up in a currency crisis? And what about stocks, bonds, and cash? The answer in each case contains a lot of "ifs" and "other things being equal," but since just about everyone owns some combination of these assets, their future is important. So here we'll look at some of the factors that affect each asset class.

Cash: Down with the dollar. In the financial world, the term "cash" means more than just the bills in your wallet. It includes the things that can either be spent or readily converted to spendable currency, like checking accounts, money market funds, and bank CDs. Right now, all have one thing in common: They pay little or no interest. As a store of value, therefore, they depend on the dollar's buying power.

Because the dollar was inflated by only a few percentage points a year in the 1990s, and interest rates were higher then, most forms of cash more or less kept their purchasing power, at least on a pretax basis. But now, with the dollar plunging against other currencies, inflation eating into the dollar's purchasing power, and U.S. interest rates near zero, your money market fund is losing ground steadily.

Does this mean you should dispense with cash entirely? No, because ready cash is a useful thing when the situation is "fluid," as the military likes to say. But do limit the balances in your checking and money market accounts to the bare minimum, perhaps enough to cover two months of day-to-day expenses. And note that all cash is not equally safe. Bank accounts are insured by the Federal Deposit Insurance Corporation, so even if your bank fails—as many will in coming years— you'll get your money. But you may not get it right away, and while the FDIC's bureaucratic wheels are slowly turning, the value of the dollar—and your cash—could be plunging. So pay attention to the quality of the bank that holds your money, and be prepared to switch to a safer one if need be. Or, because analyzing a bank's financial strength is a challenge even for professional money managers, you may want to consider spreading your cash savings among several banks.

Be even more careful about your money market funds. These are mutual funds that contain investment-grade commercial paper—that is, the short-term obligations of major companies. But the dollar's collapse and the subsequent bursting of the U.S. credit bubble will turn a lot of investment-grade debt into junk. The commercial paper of Fannie Mae, Freddie Mac, and innumerable others in home building and consumer finance are time bombs. Money market funds with this paper are not "cash" in any sense of the word, but a very dangerous form of investment with little upside (less than 1 percent in late 2003) and considerable downside. And don't be fooled by "government" money market funds. These funds mix Treasury securities with the commercial paper of Fannie and Freddie (which are still, in the minds of gullible investors, branches of the government), which is exactly what you're trying to avoid. A better bet is a Treasury-only money fund, which owns only short-term Treasury securities. Since the Treasury can print whatever it needs, it will always be able to make its interest payments, though in steadily depreciating dollars.

Here's a representative list of Treasury-only funds:

TREASURY-ONLY MONEY MARKET FUNDS

	Symbol	Telephone	Web
American Century Capital Preservation Fund	CPFXX	800-345-2021	www.americancentury.com
Dreyfus 100% U.S. Treasury Fund	DUSXX	800-645-6561	www.dreyfus.com
Fidelity Spartan U.S. Treasury Fund	FDLXX	800-544-8888	www.fidelity.com
Schwab U.S. Treasury Money Fund	SWUXX	800-435-4000	www.schwab.com
U.S. Treasury Securities Cash Fund	USTXX	800-873-8637	www.usfunds.com
Weiss Treasury Only Money Fund	WEOXX	800-814-3045	www.tommf.com

Source: Safe Money Report, Charles Schwab

U.S. bonds: The worst possible place to be. When you buy a long-term bond, you are, in effect, lending money to the bond's issuer. They take the money and run their business or government agency, and promise to pay you a certain amount of interest each month or year (known as the bond's coupon), and then, when the bond matures, give you back your original investment. This fixed income stream has a value, which fluctuates based on both the level of interest rates and the issuer's financial strength. These are separate, often unrelated issues, so let's look at each in turn:

Long-term interest rates. When interest rates fall, a bond's coupon payments look more attractive, relatively speaking, and people are willing to pay more for it, which sends the price of the bond higher. Conversely, when interest rates rise, bond prices fall. So as the dollar's orderly decline becomes a collapse, the present value of a given long-term bond's future payments will plunge. No one in their right mind will lend dollars long-term because they'll have no way of knowing what they'll get back, which is another way of saying no one will want to buy long-term bonds. Bond prices will fall, saddling bondholders with huge losses. Recall that in the mini–currency crisis of the 1970s (a pale shadow of what's coming), interest rates both long and short term soared into the high teens. Bonds bought in the previous decade at rates of 5 percent to 8 percent had income streams that were suddenly less than half as valuable as before, and their prices fell accordingly. So the people who bought those bonds expecting a steady, safe income found themselves with paper losses of 50 percent or more, and income streams with purchasing power that was much lower than they had expected.

The financial condition of the bond issuer. The more likely a borrower is to make its payments, the more valuable, relatively speaking, a bond's income stream is. But if the issuer's financial condition deteriorates, the value of its promise to pay declines and the prices of its bonds fall. If we're right about the impact of soaring U.S. debt levels, some of today's seemingly rock-solid bond issuers, like Fannie Mae and Freddie Mac, are disasters waiting to happen. When their finances begin to deteriorate, so will the value of their bonds.

Which factor—interest rates or borrower finances—will be more important this time around? We'd bet on the former. In other words, the big problem for dollar-denominated bonds is that they're, well, *dollar-denominated.* The bond market debacle of the 1930s was one of defaults, while the dollar (which was still tied to gold) actually became more valuable, which kept interest rates low and made high-quality bonds more valuable. The coming crisis will be different, with the dollar plunging and interest rates soaring. Bondholders will thus be paid back in increasingly worthless dollars. So where in the Great Depression high-quality bonds that kept making their payments rose in value while the bonds of weaker borrowers collapsed, in the coming decade all dollar-denominated bonds will fall.

Foreign bonds: Early winners, late losers. For bonds denominated in other currencies, the scenario is, initially, a mirror image of that of U.S. bonds: As the dollar falls against the euro and yen, bonds in those currencies will become more valuable in dollar terms. So in the early stages of the currency meltdown (when it's a "dollar crisis" rather than a generalized collapse of all fiat currencies), high-quality foreign bonds will do relatively well, probably outperforming both U.S. bonds and dollar-denominated money market funds.

The best way to profit from the early relative strength of the yen, euro, and other major foreign currencies is via a good global bond fund that holds a selection of bonds from around the world. Some funds that fit this profile are listed below.

But understand that when the Dollar Disease spreads to Europe and Japan, euro- and yen-denominated bonds will go the way of their U.S. cousins. This book's focus on America's mistakes should not be seen as a vote of confidence in the world's other major countries. In some ways, they're in even worse shape. Their problems will take a little longer to manifest themselves, because their particular mistakes have resulted in slow growth and anemic consumption, leading them to buy less from the U.S. than they sell to it. The resulting trade surpluses limit the global

NO-LOAD GLOBAL BOND FUNDS

Fund	Ticker	Assets ($ mill.)	3-year Av. Ann. % Return*	Telephone	Web
American Century International Bond	BEGBX	613	13.87	800-345-2021	www.americancentury.com
Loomis Sayles Global Bond	LSGLX	243	15.20	800-633-3330	www.loomissayles.com
Managers Global Bond	MGGBX	32	11.78	800-835-3879	www.managersfunds.com
Payden Global Fixed-Income	PYGSX	147	6.29	800-572-9336	www.payden.com
PIMCO Global Bond	PADMX	1,102	11.37	888-877-4626	www.pimco.com
T. Rowe Price International Bond	RPIBX	1,178	12.20	800-638-5660	www.troweprice.com

* Through 12/31/03

Source: Morningstar, Charles Schwab

supply of euros and yen, supporting their value on foreign exchange markets and making them appear, temporarily, to be strong currencies.

Just how bad are things in Europe and Japan? Let's begin with Europe, where government spending in countries like Germany and France is far higher, as a percentage of the economy, than in the U.S. Labor laws and other "structural rigidities" are more onerous than in the U.S., making it almost impossible for private companies to respond to changes in demand by shedding workers. This quite logically keeps businesses from hiring and expanding, so French and German unemployment is about twice the U.S. level. Their pension programs and health care programs, meanwhile, are vastly more generous, causing taxes to be much higher. The net result is slow growth and mounting debt.

Under normal circumstances, this "Eurosclerosis" would be hard to solve. But soon it will become even more difficult, thanks to Europe's other problem, which is demographic. Birth rates across the continent have fallen below replacement levels, and life spans are increasing. As a result, Europe is aging far faster than the U.S., and the burden of caring for a skyrocketing population of retirees is growing correspondingly faster. So scaling back their versions of Social Security and Medicare—an absolute necessity if they want to avoid financial catastrophe—will become politically impossible as the share of people in need of them rises.

Meanwhile, Japan's demographic profile makes Europe look positively healthy. Already the world's oldest population, its combination of low birthrates, long lives, and antipathy for immigration puts it in a bind that defies solution. And after a decade of mostly futile attempts to spend its way out of a lingering deflationary recession, Japan's public debt is now about three times that of the U.S. as a percent of GDP.

As for how these bad policies and ominous demographic trends translate into worthless currencies, recall that the only reason Japan or Europe can generate even their current meager rates of growth is the willingness of U.S. consumers to buy their Hondas and BMWs. As the dollar plunges, Japanese and European goods, priced in suddenly appreciating currencies, will become prohibitively expensive for U.S. consumers, who will respond by buying U.S.-made alternatives or nothing at all. Correctly interpreting this change in buying patterns as a threat to their vital export sectors, European and Japanese leaders will respond with the only weapon they have left: monetary inflation. They'll cut interest rates and buy dollars with their currencies, flooding the world with euros and yen the way the U.S. now floods the world with dollars. The result of these "competitive devaluations" will be a death spiral for all major fiat currencies, in which European or Japanese bonds will fare as badly as their U.S. cousins.

Meanwhile, forget about emerging-market bonds. They were big winners in 2003, as the liquidity flowing out of the U.S. poured into places like Brazil and Indonesia. But these countries will suffer greatly when the U.S. stops buying their exports, and because their financial systems are so fragile, their currencies—and their bonds—will be among the big losers of the coming decade.

Real Estate: Maybe not this time. The dollar crisis of the 1970s was actually a good time to own a house. Why? Because when currencies are losing value, investors rationally convert them into real assets as fast as possible.

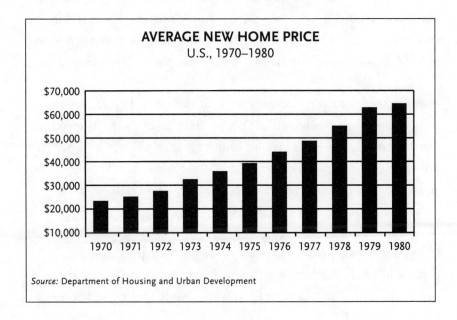

AVERAGE NEW HOME PRICE
U.S., 1970–1980

Source: Department of Housing and Urban Development

And nothing is more real than land and buildings. As the old saying goes, God is done making land. As you can see from the chart on the previous page, U.S. home prices held up well while the dollar was plunging.

Meanwhile, the people who bought homes with fixed-rate mortgages won twice, first because their homes went up in dollar terms, and second because the real—that is, adjusted for inflation—value of their mortgages plunged. This is the flip side of the bond story: When you owe money in a currency crisis, your payments are in depreciating dollars, lightening your burden a little each month. Housing, in short, was a fairly effective hedge against inflation the last time it mattered.

So there's a case to be made that real estate is another welcoming port in the coming storm. And certainly, in an environment where the dollar is losing value, a lot of capital now in financial assets will flow into buildings and land, propping up their value. But in some other very important ways, this isn't the 1970s. To put it bluntly, by virtually every measure, today's housing market is a classic financial bubble. Consider:

Prices are sky-high. In the early 1970s, the average California home cost a little more than $100,000, or not far from what the average California family's income could buy. By the end of 2003, the average California home cost $400,000, while the average family's paycheck was enough to cover a mortgage only half that size. You'll find the same trends in Boston, most of New York and Florida, and many other parts of the country.

Home equity is at a record low. Back in the early 1970s, Americans owned about 70 percent of their homes. That is, our parents owed the banks on average only 30 percent of their homes' value. But as we buy ever-larger homes and borrow against their appreciated value, home equity is shrinking. Today, Americans owe their banks nearly half of their homes' value, more than ever before.

Mortgage rates are about as low as they can go. After peaking at nearly 17 percent in 1981, the rate on a 30-year fixed-rate mortgage fell below 6 percent in 2003. This plunge in borrowing costs has enticed a whole generation of Americans to buy the biggest possible home and treat their existing homes like banks, borrowing against them to take advantage of these excitingly cheap rates. But rates are unlikely to go lower and, as we've said a few dozen times so far, will probably spike when the dollar's orderly decline becomes a death spiral. The cost of homeownership (a big part of which depends on mortgage interest rates) will then soar.

Homeowner debt is at unsustainable levels. In 1980, Americans carried a little less than a trillion dollars of mortgage debt, which came to about $20,000 per family of four. Today, we carry nearly $7 trillion, or nearly $100,000 per family of four. If you add in all the other debt in the system—government, business, credit card—the total comes to around $500,000 per family of four. Clearly, we're in no shape to begin a real-estate borrowing binge.

Too much capital is already tied up in our homes. It's possible to cook the effects of the past decade's real-estate bubble down to a single number, by dividing the aggregate value of our homes by our disposable income. The result is a sort of price/earnings ratio for the housing market, and as the next chart illustrates, this ratio bottomed out in the mid-1970s. Home prices were low in relation to our incomes, which allowed home prices to spike during the dollar crisis without straining family finances. In contrast, we're entering the coming dollar crisis with home values at record levels, both in real terms and compared to our incomes.

When the dollar really starts to slide, and panicked bond investors push interest rates back into double digits, people who have bought overpriced homes with adjustable-rate mortgages will respond in one of two ways: They'll cut back on everything else in order to make their mortgage payments (see the next section for the impact this change in spending patterns will have on the stock market), or they'll stop making their mortgage payments. Financially strapped homeowners will try to sell their homes and, in utter desperation, will take whatever is offered. Home prices will plunge in formerly hot markets, pulling local economies down with them—which in turn will make local homes

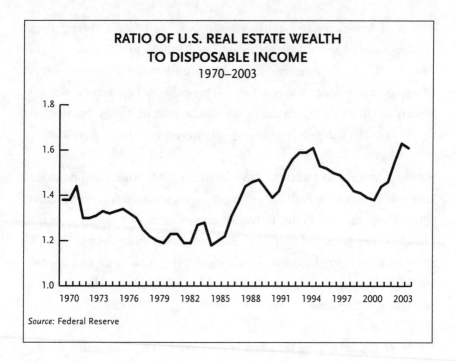

**RATIO OF U.S. REAL ESTATE WEALTH
TO DISPOSABLE INCOME**
1970–2003

Source: Federal Reserve

even less desirable. The result could be very ugly indeed in currently overheated markets like California and Boston. How ugly? In mid-2003, John Templeton, one of the most successful global money managers of the past half-century, was asked about housing in an interview. His response: "After home prices go down to one-tenth of the highest price homeowners paid, then buy."

To sum up, two very powerful opposing forces are building in the housing market: The deflation of a bursting credit bubble versus the inflation of a collapsing dollar. It's impossible to say which will win at this point, but one reasonable outcome is a tie, with home prices overall remaining steady in dollar terms, but falling dramatically versus gold. In short, your home is no longer a guaranteed hedge against inflation.

U.S. Stocks: A falling dollar equals rising exports. Here's where the analytical process gets truly complicated. Because companies come in all shapes and sizes, you'd expect some to survive and even thrive during the dollar's collapse and others to suffer right along with the greenback. The trick is telling them apart. And because of all the different factors involved, we can offer only general guidelines: First, a falling dollar helps companies that make things in the U.S. (incurring dollar-denominated expenses) for sale abroad. As the dollar falls, so do both their costs and the effective price, in yen and euro terms, of whatever they're selling. So they win twice, as their profit margins (the difference between their costs and selling prices) widen, and demand increases because of their increasingly attractive prices.

In the U.S, that means gold miners and resource companies in general, as well as commodity producers and farmers. By the end of 2003, these sectors were already booming. The long-suffering U.S. farm sector was enjoying record prices for grains and livestock, as China and India emerged as massive new markets. Farmland was suddenly a hot commodity, and farm income rose by a third in 2003, to a record $63 billion. The only thing holding farmers back was a shortage of railcars to transport their products to major ports. So look for a boom in demand for new transportation capacity in 2004 and beyond, and soaring railroad profits as they raise the rates they charge farmers desperate to get their goods to foreign markets. The same basic trends are in place for most nongold mining companies, as strong global demand for copper, zinc, etc., sends their prices soaring in dollar terms and makes U.S.-based miners a lot more profitable. The key characteristic of the industries we like best is an "inelastic supply curve," which means they're unable to quickly ramp up production of whatever they're selling. When demand surges, prices thus rise dramatically, and such companies become very profitable very fast.

U.S. manufacturers are big potential winners here too, though they require a little more analysis. Most U.S.-based exporters buy raw materials from overseas, which become more expensive as the dollar falls. And many have foreign operations that will be hurt by the host country's appreciating currency. Tracing the money flows through an entire supply chain is a little more work than the average investor is willing to put in, but, luckily, there's a shortcut: Start with a list of big manufacturers like IBM, 3M, and Procter & Gamble, which have numerous plants in the U.S. and sell many things to the global marketplace. Then check their financial statements for the effect of a weaker dollar on sales and profits. If it was highly favorable in 2002 and 2003, when the dollar fell against most other currencies, then the company's currency exposure is good for our purposes.

To find more, try a Google search under terms like "major manufacturer" and "benefits from a weaker dollar." In late 2003 a search like this would have yielded many likely prospects, including St. Jude Medical, "a $1.35 billion manufacturer of pacemakers that does about a quarter of its business in Western Europe," defense giant General Dynamics, battery maker Energizer Holdings, and auto-parts supplier Delphi. Other possibilities include U.S.-based drug makers like Merck and Pfizer and consumer products makers like Gillette, which sell globally. You'd also, we guess, have to include Ford and General Motors here, since they'll likely benefit from a rising yen's negative impact on their Japanese competitors. However, the "Big Two" have so many other problems, including massive pension liabilities and a dependence on gas-guzzling SUVs and pickups, that it's hard to see a falling dollar alone making them winners.

Another way to play this trend is through mutual funds that hold these companies. There are no pure "dollar play" stock funds out there as far as we know, but a few come close. The Buffalo USA Global Fund (BUFGX), for instance, invests in U.S. companies that derive at least 40 percent of their earnings from overseas. And Dreyfus Appreciation (DGAGX) is a low-turnover, large-cap stock fund that favors domestic companies that earn at least 35–40 percent of their income abroad. To find other similar funds, check the top holdings of these two and compare them to the holdings of other global funds.

But all bets are off when the crisis goes global. U.S. exporters and foreign bonds may do well in the early stages of a dollar crisis, but in the chaos of the later stages, when the whole concept of fiat currency is called into question, the story might be very different. As we said earlier, when the U.S. stops importing, the countries whose economies depend on our excessive spending will find themselves in trouble. Japan and China might face especially hard times, since their success depends largely on U.S. consumers' taste for inexpensive Asian imports. It's impossible to predict how these countries' leaders will react, but it's safe to say that events may, for a while, appear to be spinning out of control. So if you play the early stage of the dollar's collapse using the strategy we recommend, do it carefully and with a relatively small portion of your assets. And be prepared to sell your foreign bonds and U.S.-based manufacturing stocks when the dollar's problems begin to infect the rest of the world.

Debt: To leverage or not, that is the question. One seemingly logical strategy for profiting from a dollar collapse is to borrow as many dollars as possible, in the expectation of paying back the loans in ever-cheaper currency. A good plan in theory, perhaps, but we wouldn't advise anyone to borrow money at this point in global financial history. The fact is, leverage is beneficial only if you're absolutely, positively sure you'll be able to make the payments. If you can't, then you have problems, regardless of how right you are about trends in the foreign exchange markets. So think through your obligations and cash flow. Holding a lot of dollar cash to cover your debts is not a solution, since your cash will fall in value along with your debt. Meanwhile, unless you're a bill collector or gold miner, your job won't seem nearly as safe when the crisis is in full swing.

If you do decide to carry a fair amount of debt through the dollar crisis, make it the right kind of debt, which is fixed-rate. Under no circumstances should you load up on adjustable-rate debt, whether credit-card, mortgage, or business loans. Rates will soar when the dollar plunges, and if your financial life depends on covering a prime-plus-one loan, you'll be very unhappy when the prime rate hits 20 percent. A fixed-rate mortgage, on the other hand, is a reasonable way to borrow, since it has all the things you want in a currency crisis. It's very long-term, maybe the longest-term that's possible in today's market. It's adjustable on the downside if rates fall (through refinancing), but not on the upside if rates rise.

So how should you handle your mortgage? Depending on your circumstances, consider one of the following:

Secure your shelter. You need a roof over your head even more than you need wealth. So stop thinking of your home as an investment and start thinking of it as an essential part of your family's security. To guarantee that you come through the dollar crisis with a home to call your own, liquidate some investments and pay off your mortgage. If the dollar collapses, your home's value (assuming you haven't just bought an expensive place in a wildly overvalued neighborhood) will rise in dollar terms. And even if its resale price falls, you'll still have the shelter your house provides without the worry of a mortgage.

Leverage your home to make money. Instead of paying off your mortgage, keep it and use your free cash to buy gold and gold-based investments, as explained elsewhere in this section. In effect, you'll be borrowing against (or leveraging) your house in order to invest, with the expectation that gold will soar in dollar terms, while the real cost of your mortgage plunges. This bet paid off handsomely in the 1970s and should again in the coming decade. But it makes sense only, and we can't make this point strongly enough, *if you are certain you'll be able to make your mortgage payments.* Otherwise, it's not worth the risk.

IT WASN'T—AND WON'T BE—OPEC'S FAULT

According to most accounts of the dollar crisis of the 1970s, OPEC was the prime cause of our troubles. If those greedy sheikhs had just kept oil prices at a "reasonable" level, so goes this line of reasoning, we wouldn't have had to suffer through a decade of stagflation and all the attendant malaise. But here again, the conventional wisdom is confusing cause and effect. Just as wet streets do not cause rain, the rise of OPEC didn't cause the dollar crisis.

What really happened is that in the late 1960s and early 1970s, as you've read elsewhere in this book, the U.S. "guns and butter" policy of massive increases in government spending financed with newly printed currency led to inflation, which is another way of saying that each dollar bought less and less each year. Because the oil-producing countries priced their oil in dollars for international trade, and the dollar price of oil had been more or less stable for years, the real price of oil (that is, the purchasing power of the dollars received for each barrel) was falling sharply. OPEC ministers complained about this price erosion both publicly and privately but were unable to affect U.S. policy, which, between the Vietnam War and the Great Society, was on inflationary autopilot.

So, when the 1973 Israeli-Arab war came along, it provided political cover for OPEC to do what it really wanted to do for economic reasons: raise the dollar price of oil to recoup lost purchasing power. If you look at a chart of inflation-adjusted oil prices (or the oil/gold chart on page 42), you'll see that oil didn't actually soar in real terms in the 1970s. It fell prior to 1974 and then caught up. True, OPEC overshot the mark at first, raising prices a little more than necessary to offset the dollar's fall. But recall that it had several years of diminished purchasing power to recoup. Over the course of the decade, the net result of OPEC's price increase was about the same amount of real revenue as if the dollar had held its purchasing power and oil prices had remained stable.

As for why this matters today, as with so many other things, the oil market is repeating the 1970s pattern. Between 2000 and 2003, the dollar price of oil was more or less stable, but the dollar lost about a third of its value versus the major currencies and gold. OPEC, as a result, saw the real price of its oil cut by a similar amount and was getting antsy. In late 2003, OPEC and Russia (a large non-OPEC oil producer) were contemplating pricing oil in terms of euros for European sales, and of moving some of their investment capital out of dollars and into other currencies and gold. The upshot: As the dollar's decline accelerates, expect another oil shock, with producers raising their dollar price to recover their lost purchasing power. It will look like a price increase, and may be interpreted as an attack on the U.S. economy, but it will be neither of those things. In reality, it will be simply the market reacting quite rationally to the ongoing destruction of the dollar.

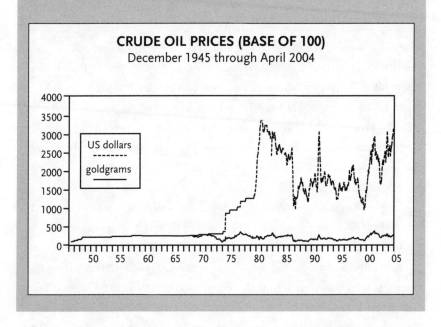

CRUDE OIL PRICES (BASE OF 100)
December 1945 through April 2004

Chapter 18

AGGRESSIVE STRATEGIES

History teaches that monetary instability can intensify with frightening speed. We wouldn't be surprised to see gold, currently around $400, blow past $600 in the coming year and then, with the whole world in a fiat-currency panic, just keep on going. In other words, we're entering a time when placing aggressive bets on the coming crisis might pay off. But before we go any further, let's make one thing very clear: Aggressive bets of any kind come with the potential for big losses—otherwise they'd be conservative, wouldn't they? This chapter's strategies are clearly in that high-risk category, which means they aren't for everyone. There is peace of mind to be gained through straight gold ownership, and plenty of money to be made in mining stocks bought and held. But for the small percentage of readers with the stomach for risk, this, as we said, is a rare chance to be on the right side of an historic realignment of the financial stars. Here's how:

SHORT SELLING: BETTING AGAINST THE DOLLAR'S VICTIMS

If some stocks will do relatively well when the dollar collapses, then many more will get creamed. Obviously, you'll want to kick them out of your portfolio. But you can also make money from their declines by actively betting against them.

The term for anticipating a decline in prices is short selling, and it works as follows: You identify a company (we'll give some criteria shortly) that seems likely to be hurt by a plunging dollar, call your broker or log on to their Web site, and sell some of the company's shares. The broker then borrows the requisite number of shares from another client's account and sells them, depositing the cash in your account. Once the stock goes down, you cover your short position by buying back the shares at their new, lower price and pocketing the difference.

Shorting is very clean and simple, with just a few complications. First, it can be done only in an account that is authorized for it, which means you'll have to set this up in advance with your broker by signing an extra contract that discloses, among other things, the risks involved in shorting stocks. If the stock you short pays dividends, they're your responsibility, adding a bit to the cost of holding a short position. A stock can be shorted only after it has gone up (the uptick rule), to prevent aggressive players from shorting stocks all the way down to zero. And finally, the risk/reward calculus of shorting is the opposite of going long: Your maximum upside is the potential downside of the stock, and since a stock can fall only to zero, 100 percent is the most you can make. But your downside is the stock's upside potential, which is theoretically unlimited, so short positions have to be watched very closely. If your positions move against you (that is, if the stocks you short go up), your broker might demand more money to cover the potential risk. This is known as a margin call, and if the money isn't quickly forthcoming, the broker will close out your short position and/or sell other shares in your account to raise the needed cash.

The juiciest short candidates fall into three general categories:

Consumer finance companies. This broad category includes banks, credit-card companies, and mortgage lenders, all of which are owed big bucks by their customers. This, as you know, is the worst possible situation in a dollar collapse.

There are two forces at work in the financial sector, which won't necessarily (in fact, probably won't) progress at the same rate. First and most obvious, the dollar-denominated cash flow that lenders earn becomes less valuable as the dollar falls. Second, the assets themselves—that is, the banks' loan portfolios—become questionable as the economy weakens, thus leading to write-offs that further reduce banks' already weakened dollar-denominated cash flow.

These two outcomes are interrelated but may not happen at the same time. For example, if people get nervous about holding dollars, many will buy goods or services, thinking that they're better off spending their dollars to take advantage of their current purchasing power rather than waiting to realize that purchasing power in the future. Thanks to this burst of spending, the economy may appear to be doing well for a time even while the dollar's problems are growing (2004's "recovery" being a case in point). If the economy is growing, people will not be losing their jobs and will, for the most part, be able to service their debts. So despite a weakening dollar, loan defaults will be modest, and loan portfolios will be profitable. However, as the dollar's problems (and the resulting higher interest rates) cause the economy to shrink and people start losing their jobs, the loans on bank balance sheets will become "value impaired." The result of this double whammy will be catastrophic for the earnings and market values of most finance companies.

For specific short candidates, it's hard to know where to start, since each part of the consumer finance business is so deeply into late-stage credit-bubble excess that a disaster is almost guaranteed. Major banks are shifting away from business loans and toward consumer lending on mortgages and credit cards, precisely the wrong thing to do at this point in the cycle. The mortgage insurers like Fannie, Freddie, and MBIA are now dependent, not just for their profitability but their survival, on low interest rates and continued consumer borrowing. And the credit-card companies—well, suffice it to say that any industry this desperate to give zero-percent loans to virtually anyone is as good as dead.

Home builders. This business used to be regional, with a given area served by a handful of local contractors who borrowed from local banks and built homes for local citizens. But in the housing boom of the

1990s, the largest home builders went national, expanding into hot markets around the country and tapping the global credit markets for effectively unlimited funds. By 2003, Wall Street's more credulous analysts were saying that these companies had transcended the old regional boom-and-bust housing cycle and would grow steadily forever after. That's patently absurd. All the nationalization of housing finance has done is guarantee that the next housing downturn will be bigger than any since the 1930s. And the home builders, valued in early 2004 as if the next housing crash will never come, are about as close to sure things as a short seller is likely to find.

Importers. If the best profile in a dollar collapse is a company that makes things here and sells them there, then the mirror image would be a logical short candidate. Japanese manufacturers like Sony and Toyota, for instance, are great companies, but highly dependent on U.S. consumers being able to afford their cars and high-definition TVs. U.S. retailers that have grown fat using overvalued dollars to buy cheap foreign goods also stand to suffer. In this category would be consumer electronics chains like Best Buy and Circuit City, which sell mostly foreign-made gadgets, along with, believe it or not, Wal-Mart, which has built an empire on cheap Chinese goods. These companies aren't quite the sure things that banks and home builders are, but they will no doubt face a margin squeeze in a dollar collapse.

As you can see, the U.S. stock market is a target-rich environment for the short seller. To get you started, on the next page you'll find fifteen possibilities, drawn from a late-2003 list of companies being shorted by the Prudent Bear fund, whose manager, David Tice, understands the impact of a falling dollar.

(Dollar) cash is trash. "Cash," as you know, can mean lots of different things. But here we're talking specifically about dollars, whether the bills in your pocket or the balance in your checking account or money market fund. Where not so long ago a big dollar cash balance was a good thing for both individuals and companies, a dollar collapse turns this

SHORT-SALE CANDIDATES

Company	Symbol	Business	Price 1/21/04	Yield %	Market Cap ($billions)
Ambac Financial	ABK	Credit insurer	74.72	0.59	7.98
American Express	AXP	Credit-card issuer	50.40	0.80	64.82
Bank of America	BAC	Money center bank	38.96	4.00	118.0
Capital One Fin.	COF	Credit-card issuer	69.85	0.16	16.13
Centex	CTX	Home builder	106.73	0.16	53.38
Citigroup	C	Money center bank	80.32	2.47	240.0
Countrywide Fin.	CFC	Mortgage lender	37.85	0.59	19.20
Fannie Mae	FNM	Mortgage insurer	59.49	1.70	74.06
Freddie Mac	FRE	Mortgage insurer	40.10	1.10	62.31
JP Morgan Chase	JPM	Money center bank	46.49	1.27	139.3
Lennar	LEN	Home builder	63.30	1.48	9.12
MBIA INC	MBI	Mortgage insurer	26.86	0.59	8.17
MBNA	KRB	Credit-card issuer	74.72	0.59	30.82
Providian	PVN	Credit-card issuer	13.25	—	3.84
Wells Fargo	WFC	"Superregional" bank	57.58	3.14	97.78

logic on its head by making cash less valuable and dollar-denominated debt less onerous.

For publicly traded companies, a big cash balance (once a good reason to buy a stock) isn't yet a screaming sell signal, but it is a red flag. The table on page 178 lists some U.S. companies with a lot of cash. They're all great firms, which is how they got so liquid in the first place, but now they face the interesting challenge of managing this money in an environment when it will become dramatically less valuable.

A good example of how a cash-rich company should operate going forward is Berkshire Hathaway, the investment vehicle of Warren Buffett, probably the greatest living money manager. As the stock market soared in the 1990s, Buffett, unable to find cheap companies to buy up, allowed cash to accumulate and by the end of 2002 was sitting on around $20 billion. Then, in a late-2003 Fortune magazine interview, he dropped a bombshell: "Through the spring of 2002, I had lived nearly 72 years without purchasing a foreign currency," he said. But now Berkshire Hathaway has made "significant investments" in other currencies. "To hold other currencies," said Buffett, "is to believe that the dollar will decline."

It's also possible that Buffett is buying gold, since he's reportedly one of the world's biggest holders of silver. He hasn't disclosed which other currencies he holds, but this fact is almost irrelevant, since all the currencies of industrialized countries are rising against the dollar. So while we wouldn't go so far as to call Microsoft and Cisco short candidates because of their U.S. dollar cash balances, if you own them or are considering owning them, their cash-management practices should be a key consideration.

Dollar debt is (maybe) a good bet. On the liability side of the ledger, the analysis is a little trickier. A company with a lot of yen- or euro-denominated debt is obviously in trouble, since the real value of its obligations will soar when the dollar falls. Conversely, a company with dollar-denominated debt will see its real liabilities fall in the coming decade, which is a good thing. But as with an individual, this improving balance sheet has to be weighed against the risk that debt presents. If higher interest rates cause a company's operating earnings to fall faster than its real interest costs, then its survival is threatened. So leverage, to be a successful strategy, has to be accompanied by strong earnings in a field that is either unaffected or actually helped by a falling dollar. It seems that all roads lead to the gold miners, doesn't it?

CASH-RICH COMPANIES

Company	Ticker	Price $ 1/21/04	Market Value ($billions)	Net Cash* ($billions)
Berkshire Hathaway	BRKa	87,400	134.6	26.9
Cisco Systems	CSCO	28.60	197.4	9.2
Dell Computer	DELL	34.76	89.0	5.0
Intel	INTC	32.20	210.2	16.2
Microsoft	MSFT	28.32	306.0	51.6

* Cash minus all debt, 12/31/03
Source: Yahoo! Finance, company annual reports

ETF Sector Fund	Symbol
iShares Dow Jones U.S. Real Estate Index	IYR
Merrill Lynch Regional Bank HOLDR Index	RKH
iShares Dow Jones U.S. Financial Services	IYG
iShares Dow Jones U.S. Financial Sector	IYF
Select Sector SPDR Fund—Financial	XLF

Source: NASDAQ

Shorting ETFs. Shorting an individual stock means taking on a level of risk that is theoretically unlimited, no small thing for an individual with limited capital. Luckily, in the same way that traditional mutual funds allow investors to limit risk by spreading their capital over many stocks, a variation on the mutual fund called an exchange-traded fund, or ETF, offers the same benefit to short sellers. An ETF is a mutual fund that is designed to trade like a stock. It can be shorted just like an individual stock (more easily, in fact, because it isn't subject to the uptick rule). So instead of shorting, say, JP Morgan Chase individually and running the risk that it somehow thrives while the rest of the banking system tanks, you can instantly spread your risks over the whole sector with a single trade by shorting a financial services ETF. Above are five that should be very profitable shorts in a dollar collapse.

Bear market mutual funds. This rare breed of mutual fund is designed to go up when the market—or some part of the market—goes down. They do this in a variety of ways, from shorting selected stocks to creating complex webs of derivatives designed to move inversely to specific stock indexes. Because some stocks will do better than others in a dollar collapse, shorting the broad indexes isn't the wisest move. So focus on the actively managed bear funds that are short the stocks you would short if you had that kind of capital. A good example is the previously mentioned Prudent Bear fund, which not only shorts the stocks of vulnerable sectors like home building and consumer finance, but owns a good bit of gold as well.

ACTIVELY MANAGED BEAR FUNDS

Fund	Ticker	Load/ no load	Telephone	Web
Comstock Part. Cap. Val.	DRCVX	Load	800-422-3554	www.comstockfunds.com
Comstock Part. Strat.	CPFAX	Load	800-422-3554	www.comstockfunds.com
Prudent Bear	BEARX	No load	888-778-2327	www.prudentbear.com
Leuthold Grizzly Short	GRZZX	No load	800-273-6886	www.leutholdfunds.com

Source: Morningstar, fund Web sites

REALLY GOING FOR IT: MARGIN AND OPTIONS

Margin. As you build your portfolio of gold-mining shares, you're also building collateral. That is, you're creating an asset against which you can borrow to buy more shares. This kind of debt is called margin, and it works like this: Say that you buy shares of Newmont Mining worth $50,000, which uses up all the cash in your brokerage account. Then you buy $25,000 of Goldcorp shares. Your broker will loan you the money, using your Newmont shares as collateral, and charge you a nominal interest rate, called the margin rate. You now control 50 percent more gold-mining shares than you could have without borrowing. If gold soars and your stocks rise, you earn more profit than had you simply been fully invested.

The table on page 181 illustrates the potential profit differential. Note that in both cases you start with the same amount of capital. The margined portfolio just leverages it more aggressively.

Margin, like any other form of leverage, brings time into the equation, in the sense that a margined bet has to be right not only about where a given stock will end up but about how it behaves along the way. If gold goes down in 2005 and soars in 2006, a buy-and-hold investor does just fine. But a margined account has a potential problem, because the size of its paper losses in 2005 will be magnified by its leverage. If the value of

THE IMPACT OF MARGIN ON PORTFOLIO RETURNS

Unmargined Portfolio		Margined Portfolio	
	Profit		Profit
Newmont*	$50,000	Newmont*	$50,000
		Goldcorp†	$25,000
Total Profit	$50,000	Total Profit	$75,000‡

*1,000 shares bought at $50 per share and sold at $100
†1,785 shares bought on margin at $14 and sold at $28
‡Excluding interest and transaction costs

your margin account shrinks beyond a certain point, your broker will ask for more money—known as a margin call—and, as with a short sale, if you aren't forthcoming he'll simply sell off the stocks in your account at the prevailing price. Your paper loss will become real, and you'll miss out on the chance to profit from gold's subsequent bull market. Margin is a very dangerous tool, in other words, so before using it, lay down some hard-and-fast rules. Bet only money that you can afford to lose. Margin only a small part of your capital and watch the position closely. Decide on the maximum loss you can tolerate and be prepared to scale back when you reach this limit. The last thing you want is to be on the sidelines due to margin calls when the gold train leaves the station.

Options. An option is a contract that gives its owner the right, but not the obligation, to buy or sell a specified number of shares at a predetermined price within a set time period. Call options allow a holder to buy (i.e., call away) shares, and puts confer the right to sell (or put the shares into someone else's account). They're "derivatives" in the sense that their value is derived from that of an underlying security, most frequently the stock of a publicly traded company (though options exist for lots of other things). Stock option contracts control 100 shares of the underlying stock, so a quoted price (or premium) of, say, $2 implies a cost of $200 for a given contract. Because you're paying only for the right to profit from a change in the stock's price, you pay a lot less than if you bought the entire hundred shares outright. Yet you gain, if you're right, almost as much as if you owned the shares.

LEAPS. Traditional options have one huge drawback: They're short-lived. Most run for nine months or less, so unless you're right on both direction and timing, that call you bought with such high hopes will expire worthless, and you'll lose everything you paid for it. In response, the options exchanges have built a better mousetrap, called LEAPS, or Long-Term Equity AnticiPation Securities. These are options with life spans of up to two and a half years, allowing you to be fuzzy on "when" but still make money from a gold explosion in, say, 2006. You pay more for the extra time but still get more bang for the speculative buck than with margin, while limiting your risk to the option purchase price.

Using Newmont, whose LEAPS are actively traded, as an example, take a look at the table on page 183. The LEAPS calls listed there appeared in Yahoo! Finance on November 25, 2003. They expire on January 20, 2006, giving their holders a little over two years in which to be right. The open interest column indicates the number of contracts that have been bought and are still outstanding. Note that some have very little open interest, while others have a lot, indicating the market's perception of which are most attractive.

Since option players have bought nearly as many 55s as all the others put together, let's use them for our example. The premium on this call is $6.80, or $680 for a contract controlling 100 shares. A strike price of $55 means that the stock has to rise above this level for the option to be "in the money," or exercisable at a profit. Add in the premium of $6.80 and a modest commission, and a holder of this option will need a price of $62 on Newmont stock to break even. With the stock at $45 on the day in question, that requires a 50-percent increase. What are the odds of this? We'd say pretty good, but that's something you'll have to decide for yourself before choosing this strategy.

The table on page 184 shows how this LEAPS call will perform under two scenarios, one where Newmont doesn't move for the next

LEAPS CALL OPTIONS, NEWMONT MINING

Expiration date January 20, 2006

Strike	Symbol	Last	Bid	Ask	Open Interest
10.00	WIEAB.X	0.00	35.70	36.00	128
15.00	WIEAC.X	27.70	31.00	31.40	77
20.00	WIEAD.X	0.00	26.60	27.10	38
25.00	WIEAE.X	22.00	22.50	23.00	764
30.00	WIEAF.X	17.60	18.80	19.30	552
35.00	WIEAG.X	15.20	15.50	15.90	402
40.00	WIEAH.X	12.60	12.60	13.00	659
45.00	WIEAI.X	10.20	10.10	10.50	932
50.00	WIEAJ.X	8.60	8.10	8.40	1,473
55.00	WIEAK.X	6.70	6.60	6.80	4,257
60.00	WIEAL.X	0.00	5.20	5.40	505
65.00	WIEAM.X	4.30	4.10	4.40	4
80.00	WIEAP.X	2.20	2.10	2.25	390

All prices as of November 25, 2003
Source: NASDAQ

two years, and the other where it goes to $100 a share. Note that because the option is a wasting asset that becomes less valuable as time goes on, and then worthless if it expires out of the money, in the first scenario the options player loses all $680, or 100 percent of his investment, while the stockholder breaks even (actually earning a little bit if Newmont pays dividends). In the optimistic scenario, the stock soars, giving the shareholder a gain of a little more than 100 percent. But the LEAPS holder does just a tad better, breaking even at $62, and then racking up $3,800 profit, or a gain of nearly 500 percent. And they do so while risking only $680, versus $4,500 for the shareholder. Now you see how leverage works, and what options players stand to gain if gold does what we expect in the next few years.

Volatility spreads. Now let's say you have no doubt that the gold market will be thrilling over the next couple of years but aren't sure, at least initially, whether its fundamentals will send it higher or central-bank manipulation will force it lower. Options allow you to place a bet that wins either way.

	Scenario One: The stock just sits there		Scenario Two: The stock runs from $45 to $100	
	Profit $	% gain (loss)	Profit $	% gain
Stockholder*	0	0	$5,500	60
Call holder†	(680)	(100)	$3,800	500

*$100 shares purchased at $45. Total funds risked: $4,500.
†One Jan. 20, 2006, $55 LEAPS call, purchased for $680.

Simply buy both a call and a put on a major gold stock, so that you profit from a big move in either direction, and lose only if the stock just sits there. With this kind of "volatility spread," you have to shift mental gears a bit and think of volatility (or "vol," as traders call it) as the thing you're buying and selling, rather than a given stock. Your break-even point is the combined cost of the two options, and once one of the options moves far enough to offset both premiums, anything beyond that point is profit.

It's also possible to start with a straight volatility spread and then adjust it to changing circumstances by adding options to one side or the other, producing a partially hedged bet on a given scenario. To illustrate, if you start with one call and one put, and you begin to suspect that fundamentals are about to win out over the central banks, and gold therefore is about to soar, you can add another call or two, which magnifies your upside potential. If you're wrong and gold falls, the remaining put will partially offset the falling value of your calls.

This brief overview just scratches the surface of possible options strategies. Once you dig into them, you'll find ways to generate income from a slow-moving stock (covered call writing) and lock in profits without selling (collars), among many other things, some of which will come in handy as the dollar crisis unfolds. But none are as simple as they seem. Because options come with a variety of strike prices, each with its own time value and premium, their relative attractiveness is constantly shifting, and it takes considerable sophistication to tell best from worst. So before venturing beyond simple puts and calls, take advantage of some of the options resources that are freely available. The Options

Industry Council offers a free tutorial CD, available by calling 888-OPTIONS, that walks viewers through the various strategies, from the simplest to the most ornate. And the Council's call center, says Council president Paul Stevens, is staffed with knowledgeable people "who are available to play 'stump the expert.'" Your broker, meanwhile, almost certainly offers some combination of tutorials and personal advice.

Chapter 19

TWENTY-FIRST CENTURY GOLD

The strategies we've sketched out so far will probably outperform stocks, bonds, and real estate in the coming decade. But none are perfect. Bullion coins and small bars can be expensive, with markups and related insurance/storage charges approaching 10 percent of the value of the gold content. Rare coins cost far more than their constituent metal and, like bullion, can be inconvenient and expensive to store.

Gold-mining stocks, meanwhile, are partially dependent on non-gold factors like the wisdom of company managers and the stability of the countries where their mines are located. Traditional actively managed precious-metals mutual funds can be purchased only after the market closes, generally have very high expense ratios, and aren't suitable for trading. And both stocks and bullion are vulnerable to a panicked government's attempts at confiscation, nationalization, or other restrictions on their trading or liquidity.

You'd think that by now the precious-metals world would have come up with some better ways to own gold. And you'd be right. Several new gold-based products have either been introduced in the past few years or will be soon. Each, if done right, has advantages over today's alternatives, and though none have gone mainstream as this is written in early

2004, all should be available soon. Between them they promise to revolutionize the gold market. Here are two that stand out:

Gold-exchange-traded funds. ETFs, as you'll recall from Chapter 18, are mutual funds with an interesting twist. They generally hold a basket of stocks from a given market index or industry, like a traditional fund, but they trade like a stock. You can buy or sell an ETF with a phone call or mouse click, and you can short them as you can IBM or Microsoft. They allow you to set limit and stop-loss orders to protect yourself during times of market volatility. And because an ETF's basket of stocks doesn't need much care and feeding, its expense ratio is generally far lower than that of the average actively managed fund. The Standard & Poor's Depository Receipts ETF, for instance, matches the S&P 500 Index but charges only .12 percent a year, versus .76 percent for Fidelity Magellan, the largest actively managed stock fund. To sum up, an ETF combines the diversification of a mutual fund with the trading ease of a common stock.

The ETF concept is tailor-made for both physical gold and gold-mining shares, and for the past few years the World Gold Council (WGC), the mining industry's trade organization, has been trying to bring a bullion ETF to market. As envisioned, the WGC's ETF will hold a vault full of gold bars, offering investors the chance to own real gold rather than just the promise of a bank or mint to pay gold upon request. The fund will trade like a stock on a U.S exchange and have expenses in the 0.5-percent-per-year range, far less than other alternatives for buying and storing physical gold. Its only conceptual drawback is that gains generated by its appreciation might be taxed as regular income rather than as capital gains.

Similar ETFs now trade in Australia and England, but unfortunately, the concept has yet to be perfected in the U.S. In May 2003, the WGC submitted to the Securities & Exchange Commission (SEC) the S-1 registration statement required to obtain approval for a New York Stock Exchange listing. But the SEC sent the WGC back to the drawing board. In the ensuing eight months, the WGC submitted two amended S-1s, neither of which, as this is written in January 2004, has been accepted.

What's the problem? Neither the SEC nor the WGC is talking. But a detailed reading of the WGC's most recent SEC filing, as well as the prospectus for its London ETF, reveals a surprising number of possibilities. In a nutshell, the WGC funds have very loose custodial controls. That is, the language of the agreement leaves open the possibility that the funds have less than total control over their gold, so that investors might end up owning less gold than they think. For example, the funds' structure allows its managers to contract out storage of its gold to subcustodians. And though it requires the custodian (i.e., the bank hired by the WGC to store the fund's gold) to use "reasonable care" in the selection of those subcustodians, it explicitly absolves the custodian of liability for "any act or omission, or for the solvency, of any subcustodian it appoints unless the appointment of that subcustodian was made by it negligently or in bad faith." In plain English, the people storing the funds' gold aren't being supervised the way they should be. Shares purchased by investors, as a result, may not be backed by physical gold. This is obviously a bad thing and perhaps explains the SEC's reluctance to okay the fund.

Perhaps by the time you read this, the WGC will have improved their funds' governance and its ETF will have passed SEC muster and be trading on a U.S. exchange. If so, give it serious consideration, because structured correctly, such an ETF will be an easy way to own physical gold.

Digital gold. Gold's soaring exchange rate won't, by itself, make the metal a viable currency. Regardless of how many dollars a gram of it is worth, bullion still suffers from the imperfections that led to the creation of paper money in the first place: A pocketful of gold is bulky, heavy, and noisy, and a gold coin still wears out as it passes from hand to hand, a subtle but pernicious form of debasement.

But those problems are about to be solved, thanks, believe it or not, to the Internet. Now that electronic payment systems have reduced the concept of money to its essence, which is information, most fund transfers are simply electronic debits and credits, and most of our getting and spending is now via credit cards, online checking accounts, and (soon) payment-enabled cell phones. We no longer touch most of our currency, making its actual form, whether paper, metal, or virtual, irrelevant.

For gold, the digitization of money leads to a conclusion that's both profound and quite logical: If money is a means of communication, and the Internet is the world's most powerful communications medium, then the Internet can allow gold to circulate as currency, making it once again the world's common language for economic calculation. Convert gold into bits, in other words, and you've retained all its strengths as money while eliminating its weaknesses as currency.

Conceptually, "digital gold" works like this: You transfer some dollars or euros or whatever to a firm (the currency manager) that has deposited gold bars in a super-safe vault. The currency manager credits your account with the requisite weight of gold, and you then make payments from this account via your computer. The gold—without ever leaving the vault—is debited from your account and credited to the recipient's.

The first attempt to put this theory into practice is called E-Gold, and its early results illustrate both digital gold's potential and its pitfalls. Between 1999 and 2002, with virtually no marketing, the number of E-Gold accounts rose from 3,000 to 350,000. The amount of E-Gold in circulation (which by definition is identical to the amount of gold locked away in the vaults used by Gold & Silver Reserve, the currency's manager) grew from 5,000 ounces to 60,000 ounces, or approximately the annual output of a medium-sized gold mine.

But since then, the amount of E-Gold in circulation has declined. What happened? Several things, including the failure of two gold-based payment systems, one of which was closely aligned to E-Gold by some common ownership and directors, and the fraud conviction of Gold & Silver Reserve's largest outside investor. By 2003, the momentum had shifted to another digital currency invented by James called GoldMoney (www.goldmoney.com). Because James is the founder of GoldMoney, we face an obvious conflict of interest in discussing it. So while we expect some form of digital gold to play a major, if not leading, role in tomorrow's monetary system, in the paragraphs that follow we're using GoldMoney simply as an example of how digital gold works, not recommending its purchase.

A goldgram account at GoldMoney functions like a garden-variety checking account, except that instead of an electronic book entry at a bank, an account holder owns actual gold, stored in a "treasury-grade," insured vault in London. Instead of dollars, the unit of account, as the name implies, is one goldgram, or about 3.2 percent of an ounce of gold. The penny's role is played by the mil, equal to one-thousandth of a goldgram. Account holders spend their money (note that we're able to call this currency "money" because, unlike the dollar, it is a tangible asset) by going online, specifying a recipient and an amount, and hitting "enter." There's a fee of 1 percent per transaction, up to a maximum of 100 mils (about $1.28 at $400 per ounce) each time you make a payment. There is also a monthly account fee of 100 mils, similar to the fee charged by a bank for providing your checking account.

Digital gold enables its holders to keep part of their "cash" in gold rather than dollars, avoiding the dollar's loss of purchasing power while still being able to buy things. As this is written in early 2004, dozens of merchants in the precious-metals world, including most of the newsletters listed at the back of this book, accept digital gold. Meanwhile, with a markup only 2–3 percent above the spot gold price, goldgrams are far cheaper to purchase than other forms of bullion.

Again, we're not suggesting that you run out and convert all your dollar cash to digital gold. The concept is so new, for one thing, that the tax consequences of spending this kind of money are unknown as of this writing. But we recommend that you keep an eye on the field, because, done right, these currencies answer at least two problems now facing gold owners: how to own physical gold, and how to hold cash without being exposed to depreciating dollars.

As both a viable medium of exchange and a store of value, digital gold offers something the world hasn't seen since the 1930s—a functioning gold currency. And its rise might have a profound impact on the gold market by standing the traditional currency supply/demand equation on its head. Consider: If the Fed creates more dollars, the value of each individual dollar tends, other things being equal, to go down. But when someone opens a digital gold account, the currency's manager buys gold and stores it. This increased demand puts upward pressure on gold's exchange rate. So *the more digital gold that's created, the more valuable it becomes.*

Now suppose that gold continues to rise as we've forecast, making each unit of digital gold more valuable, and the currency itself a vastly better store of value than dollars. Seeing this, more people might begin shifting money into digital gold, causing demand for gold to rise and further boosting its exchange rate, and so on, in a positive feedback loop that sends gold through the roof.

Chapter 20

HOW MUCH GOLD SHOULD YOU OWN?

Ask the average financial planner about precious metals, and you'll get the conventional answer: Put most of your money in stocks, bonds, and cash, and no more than 10 percent into gold as a "hedge" against the highly unlikely event of financial instability. But as you've no doubt gathered, we view this traditional asset-allocation strategy as wildly speculative, since cash, bonds, and many stocks are at grave risk in a dollar crisis. Instead, you're better off putting not just a bit, but the bulk, of your cash into physical gold and most of the rest of your capital into gold-related investments. How much? Again, that depends on your needs, temperament, and objectives, but the logic is essentially a mirror image of the traditional approach: The more conservative you are, the more gold you should own. Put another way, when the dollar is collapsing, the asset most likely to hold (i.e., preserve) its value is gold. So if preservation of capital is the goal, then you should own physical gold for liquidity, along with investments in the shares of unhedged majors and/or the mutual funds that own them. More-aggressive investors can hold mining stocks with greater leverage, along with silver, foreign bond funds, and mutual funds specializing in U.S.-based resource and manufacturing companies. And the most adventurous should focus on smaller miners, the shares of U.S.-based manufacturers, gold-based derivatives, and short positions in financial stocks.

Hold just enough dollar cash to cover your day-to-day bills, since its value will decline, if not evaporate. Avoid U.S. bonds and anything else with a payment stream denominated in dollars. And stay away from future trouble spots like the shares of consumer finance companies. No matter how conservative they look, in the coming decade they'll be anything but. Here are a few possible ways of turning these principles into portfolios:

MODEL PORTFOLIOS

Conservative	% of total capital
Dollar cash	5
Gold bullion	40
Precious-metals mutual funds and unhedged gold-mining companies	30
Foreign bond funds	25

Moderate	% of total capital
Dollar cash	5
Gold bullion	20
Silver bullion	10
Shares of unhedged majors and high-quality mid-tiers	35
Foreign bond funds	15
No-load funds specializing in U.S.-based resource/ manufacturing companies	15

Aggressive	% of total capital
Dollar cash	2
Gold and silver bullion	18
Unhedged gold-mining majors	20
Shares of emerging mid-tiers, juniors, and property plays	35
Short positions in U.S. consumer finance companies	20
Long-term call options on mining shares	5

THE CONFISCATION THREAT

By now we know a few things about governments. They do whatever it takes to keep getting bigger, they eventually destroy their currencies, and—when the crisis is finally upon them—they react by confiscating their citizens' wealth. So as we drift into yet another currency debacle, one question that should be on all of our minds is How will Washington respond? Will it freeze prices as did Nixon? Confiscate our gold like FDR? Prevent us from moving our savings to safer foreign markets and buying foreign currencies? Or come up with some ingenious new kind of expropriation, one tailored to the modern financial world?

There is no answer at this point, of course, because no two currency crises are exactly alike, and in any event much depends on the temperaments of the people in charge when the dollar goes into free fall. But some informed speculation is possible, along with a few general guidelines for preparing. So let's begin with another look at FDR's executive order, in which he declared on April 5, 1933, that "All persons are hereby required to deliver on or before May 1, 1933, to a Federal Reserve Bank or a branch or agency thereof or to any member bank of the Federal Reserve System all gold coin, gold bullion and gold certificates now owned by them."

The story told today is that our "law-abiding" grandparents willingly lined up to turn in their gold, but the real story is more interesting. The table below, based on data reported by Milton Friedman and Anna Schwartz in their book *A Monetary History of the United States, 1867–1960*, indicates that:

1. The total quantity of monetary gold (i.e., gold bullion/coin in bank vaults and circulating gold coin) in the U.S. was declining before FDR announced the confiscation on April 5. The amount of gold held by banks, the Federal Reserve, and the U.S. Treasury fell by 5.5 percent, while gold coins in circulation fell a staggering 35.5 percent in the three months prior to FDR's announcement. Why the decline? Because confiscation was widely anticipated, and some people chose to move their gold to safety—just in case the rumors turned out to be true.

2. After the confiscation announcement, only 3.9 million ounces of gold coin—approximately 21.9 percent of the gold coin then in circulation—was turned in. The government assumed, according to Friedman and Schwartz, that the remaining coins were "lost, destroyed, exported without record, or . . . in numismatic collections." After analyzing each possibility, Friedman and Schwartz concluded "that in Jan. 1934 the bulk of the [remaining coin] was retained illegally in private hands."

If the goal of confiscation was to eliminate private gold ownership, it clearly failed. And if the goal was to restore confidence in the U.S. monetary system by increasing the amount of gold backing the dollar, the table below implies that simply devaluing the dollar would have done

MONETARY GOLD IN THE UNITED STATES

	Circulating Gold Coin (million oz.)	Gold Stock (million oz.)	$/oz.	$ Value of Gold Stock (millions)
Dec '32	27.6	204.5	$20.67	$4,226
Mar '33	17.8	193.3	$20.67	$3,995
Jan '34	13.9	195.1	$35.00	$6,829

the trick. Note how the dollar value of the U.S. gold stock soared when the dollar was redefined as $^1\!/_{35}$ of an ounce of gold. In other words, a divisive step like confiscation seems, in retrospect, totally unnecessary.

This point is so crucial that it bears closer examination. In 1933, it took 20.67 dollars to exchange for one ounce of gold. The confiscation raised the total gold stock only slightly, from 193.3 million ounces to 195.1 million. After the devaluation, it took 35 dollars, or 69.3 percent more, to exchange for an ounce of gold, and the total U.S. gold stock was worth $6,829 million, versus its predevaluation $3,995 million. Assuming that this $6,829 million total provided the right amount of gold backing needed to restore confidence in the dollar, simply devaluing the dollar by 70.9 percent instead of 69.3 percent would have made the original 193.3 million ounces worth $6,829 million.

Though a little tedious, these calculations bring us to a question that is anything but tedious: If the confiscation was unnecessary, why did FDR do it? Clearly, he had an objective that was unrelated to the immediate value of the dollar. But what was it? One possibility is examined in a 1966 essay titled "Gold and Economic Freedom," written by, of all people, Alan Greenspan:

> The abandonment of the gold standard made it possible for the welfare statists to use the banking system as a means to an unlimited expansion of credit. . . . The financial policy of the welfare state requires that there be no way for the owners of wealth to protect themselves. This is the shabby secret of the welfare statists' tirades against gold. Deficit spending is simply a scheme for the confiscation of wealth. Gold stands in the way of this insidious process. It stands as a protector of property rights. If one grasps this, one has no difficulty in understanding the statists' antagonism toward the gold standard.

Leaving aside the irony of these words coming from the man who now presides over the kind of unrestrained credit expansion that he once accused "statists" of engineering, Greenspan's analysis leads to a very disturbing conclusion: If the state's imperative is to grow at whatever cost to its citizens' welfare, then in the coming crisis gold is certainly once again at risk, but not just gold. Because this time around most Americans own tax-deferred accounts, vast pools of private wealth that under current law is off-limits to tax collectors. So why stop with gold, which, as FDR discovered in 1933, is easy to hide and therefore hard to confiscate? Why not grab the easy pickings like 401(k)s and IRAs and replace them with government IOUs?

History also teaches that governments in crisis tend to nationalize the industries that are the source of their countries' wealth and/or insecurity. In a dollar collapse, that would be the gold miners, oil producers, and other resource companies. So it's at least conceivable that in the coming crisis the assets of U.S.-based miners will be seized and their shareholders paid in those same government IOUs.

How do you protect yourself from this kind of forced conversion into the one currency you really don't want to own? In a word, diversify. Spread your assets among several nations, in several forms. Own physical gold and put it beyond the government's reach. Buy the shares of mining stocks with reserves in relatively safe parts of the world. Convert some cash into digital gold, stored in a non-U.S. vault. Open Canadian, Swiss, German, or Japanese bank and brokerage accounts. And be very careful about how much of your wealth is in easy-to-freeze accounts like IRAs and 401(k)s.

Chapter 22

GOOD INFORMATION

If we've done our job, by now you should have a clear sense of the risks and opportunities presented by the dollar's collapse, and a thirst for up-to-date information. Luckily, there's plenty of good information out there. The sound money community is big, vibrant, and accessible, and in this section we've listed some of the most useful books, newsletters, and Web sites. We recommend that you become familiar with the leading theorists, past and present, and read some of their books; subscribe to at least one and preferably two or three good newsletters; and visit several of the Web sites listed here on a daily basis. If you do, nothing that happens in the next few years will surprise you.

BOOKS

The Dollar Crisis: Causes, Consequences, Cures, by Richard Duncan
Hardcover price: $29.95
A detailed look at the reasons for the dollar's coming collapse, by a former International Monetary Fund consultant.

GoldWars: The Battle Against Sound Money as Seen from a Swiss Perspective,
by Ferdinand Lips
Paperback price: $19.95
A Swiss economist's history of the abandonment of gold-as-money and
the ongoing attempts by central banks to manipulate the gold market.

Manias, Panics, and Crashes: A History of Financial Crises, by Charles P.
Kindleberger
Hardcover price: $19.95
A highly regarded historical/theoretical explanation of why financial
crises keep happening.

Extraordinary Popular Delusions and the Madness of Crowds, by Charles
MacKay
Hardcover price: $9.98
The classic history of humanity's financial bubbles. The striking thing
about MacKay's depiction of the Dutch Tulip mania and its many suc-
cessors is how familiar they seem.

The Theory of Money & Credit, by Ludwig von Mises
Hardcover price: $20.00
Human Action, by Ludwig von Mises
Paperback price: $24.95
Mises was one of the founders of the Austrian school of economics and
remains a deity in the sound-money world. These serious economics
texts are well worth the effort.

Infectious Greed: How Deceit and Risk Corrupted the Financial Markets, by
Frank Partnoy
Paperback price: $15.00
An accessible explanation of how financial engineering in general and
derivatives in particular are corrupting global capitalism.

At the Crest of the Tidal Wave: A Forecast for the Great Bear Market, by
Robert Prechter
Hardcover price: $14.99
Conquer the Crash: You Can Survive and Prosper in a Deflationary Depression,
by Robert Prechter. Hardcover price: $27.95
These books lay out, in terrifying detail, the theoretical basis for
Prechter's prediction of a deflationary depression. See our discussion of
his newsletter on page 203.

*The Case for the 100% Gold Dollar, and What Has Government Done to Our
Money?* by Murray Rothbard
Rothbard offers the libertarian take on the nature of money, and gold's
potential in tomorrow's monetary system. These, along with several of
his other books, can be downloaded free of charge from the Ludwig von
Mises Institute Web site (www.mises.org).

NEWSLETTERS (in alphabetical order)

Dow Theory Letters
Editor: Richard Russell
Since 1958
Frequency: Every three weeks
Trial subscription: Two issues for $1
Annual rate: $250
Dow Theory Letters, Inc.
P.O. Box 1759
La Jolla, CA 92038-1759
Tel: (858) 454-0481
Web site: www.dowtheoryletters.com
E-mail: staff@dowtheoryletters.com

Richard Russell gained wide recognition for a series of technical articles
in *Barron's,* beginning in 1956. He founded the *Dow Theory Letters* (*DTL*) in
1958 and has been at it ever since (never once having skipped a *Letter*).

His record speaks for itself: He recommended gold stocks way back in 1960. He called the top of the 1949–66 bull market and—almost to the day—the beginning of the bull market that started in December 1974. Hulbert Financial Digest ranks *DTL* first on a risk-adjusted basis among all market-timing newsletters over the past twenty-three years.

Published every three weeks, *DTL* covers the U.S. stock and bond markets, along with foreign markets, precious metals, and commodities. One of the most useful features of the *Letter* is Russell's daily Primary Trend Index (PTI), a proprietary index that has been an amazingly accurate predictor of near-term market moves.

Recently, Russell has become a raging gold bull (recall the quote that opens Part Three). His take is basically the same as ours: Gold is money, fiat currencies are not, and the difference will become increasingly apparent in coming years. As he noted in a recent interview, "It's simple—central banks are generating vastly more paper than the gold mines can produce in comparable gold values. . . . Now is the time to accumulate gold and gold stocks." On his seventy-ninth birthday in July 2003, he sold all his bonds, because "the U.S. is heading for maybe the greatest financial mess in world history."

Elliott Wave Theorist
Editor: Robert R. Prechter Jr.
Since 1979
Frequency: Monthly
Trial subscription: NA
Rate: $20 month
Elliott Wave International
P.O. Box 1618
Gainesville, GA 30503
Tel: (800) 336-1618 or, outside the U.S., (770) 536-0309
Fax: (770) 536-2514
Web site: www.elliottwave.com
E-mail: customerservice@elliottwave.com

Robert Prechter is the author of the best-seller *Conquer the Crash*. His analytical approach is based on the discoveries of Ralph Nelson Elliott, who in the 1930s and 1940s noticed repeating patterns in the prices of various commodities. Elliott noted that the patterns repeated on different temporal and numerical scales and seemed to reflect market participants' mental states. From this he deduced that investors go through regular, predictable mood swings, from cautious (as in the 1950s) to risk tolerant (the 1980s) to downright euphoric (the 1990s). This last stage leads to a crash, after which the cycle begins again.

The same repeating pattern governs the movement of commodities and stock prices, and in his *Elliott Wave Theorist* newsletter, Prechter analyzes these waves to generate forecasts for both near-term prices and long-term economic activity. His work is thus useful for both traders and investors, along with those who simply want a framework for understanding the modern world. And his main conclusion is that we're entering a downturn that will rival, if not surpass, the Great Depression. Gold, he says, may not do well in such a deflationary scenario. But readers should overlook this point in light of his great analysis of the big picture.

Freemarket Gold & Money Report
Editor: James Turk
Since 1987
Frequency: 20 letters annually plus occasional interim reports
Trial subscription: $60 for 3 months
Annual rate: $220 for e-mail delivery, or $260 for hard copy by mail
1857-240 White Mountain Highway
P.O. Box 5002
North Conway, NH 03860
Tel: (603) 323-8182
Fax: (603) 323-8161
Web site: www.fgmr.com
E-mail: contact@fgmr.com

The *Freemarket Gold & Money Report* offers an international perspective on the precious-metals and financial markets. Each letter provides buy and sell recommendations on gold, silver, mining stocks, stock markets, bonds, and currencies. Because this is James's newsletter, we'll refrain from commenting on it, except to note that it is one of the oldest precious-metals newsletters and deals with many of the same issues covered in this book.

Gold Mining Stock Report
Editor: Robert Bishop
Since 1983
Frequency: Approximately 50 alerts e-mailed or faxed
Trial subscription: US$250 for 3 months
Annual rate: US$1000
P.O. Box 1217
Lafayette, CA 94549
Tel: (925) 284-1165
Fax: (925) 891-9188
Web site: www.goldminingstockreport.com
E-mail: info@goldminingstockreport.com

Robert Bishop travels the world to inspect new mines and interview management teams. His goal is to discover emerging miners that go on to become big ones—or sell out to big ones at a nice profit. He succeeds consistently.

With fifty alerts per year, this is the most frequently updated newsletter on our list. Each update offers a concise rundown of current events in the gold market, along with analyses of several emerging miners.

Gold Newsletter
Editor: Brien Lundin
Since 1971
Frequency: 12 letters annually
Trial subscription: Free issue available online

Annual rate: $198
2400 Jefferson Highway
Suite 600
Jefferson, LA 70121
Tel: (800) 877-8847
Fax: (504) 837-4885
Web site: www.goldnewsletter.com
E-mail: gnlmail@jeffersoncompanies.com

Founded in 1971 as the principal tool in Jim Blanchard's fight to return the right of private gold ownership to American citizens, *Gold Newsletter* has, in its 30-plus years of continuous publication, featured contributions from many of the modern world's leading free-market economists and investment analysts.

Now edited by Blanchard's longtime partner and associate, Brien Lundin, *Gold Newsletter* focuses on mining stocks involved in exploration and preproduction but also does a good job of covering the metal markets themselves. It features guest commentary from speakers at the New Orleans Investment Conference, and its "Potpourri" section remains an industry favorite. But its main attraction is the sheer volume of its stock recommendations. The sample issue available on its Web site in early 2004 was sixteen pages long, with profiles and/or analyses of twenty-three mining stocks. In a typical issue, expect to see a few well-known names but far more new ones.

Gold Stock Analyst
Editor: John Doody
Since 1994
Frequency: Monthly
Trial subscription: Sample issue available online
Annual rate: $350
P.O. Box 7440
Ft. Lauderdale, FL 33338
Tel: Order service at (800) 237-8400, ext. 308

Web site: www.goldstockanalyst.com
E-mail: goldstock@goldstockanalyst.com

Gold Stock Analyst is so loaded with data that subscribers tend to hoard back issues and refer to them when doing further research. Each issue contains tables listing the vital statistics (earnings, production levels, production costs, and much more) for virtually every gold, silver, and platinum miner of note. Ditto for the gold market in general: Doody keeps subscribers abreast of supply/demand trends, bullion bank short positions, and the relative valuations of stocks and bullion. And then, of course, he offers detailed analyses of half a dozen or so gold miners of various sizes and profiles.

Each issue lists Doody's top ten stock picks, which generally includes a mix of majors, mid-tiers, and juniors. A recent issue, for instance, recommended majors like Anglogold and Newmont along with juniors like Crown Resources and Canyon Resources. Simply buy these stocks and you've created a diversified gold-mining portfolio that, based on past results, will do quite well. The top picks in 2003 rose by an average of 90 percent, versus 40 percent for the XAU index of major gold miners and 20 percent for gold itself.

Grant's Interest Rate Observer
Editor: James Grant
Since 1983
Frequency: 24 issues
Trial subscription: 8 for $350
Per issue download: $50
Annual rate: $760
2 Wall Street
New York, NY 10005
Tel: (212) 809-7994
Fax: (212) 809-8492
Web site: www.grantspub.com
E-mail: subscriptions@grantspub.com

James Grant founded the *Interest Rate Observer* in 1983, after an eight-year stint at *Barron's*, where he originated the "Current Yield" column. He's the author of four books on finance or financial history, including *Money of the Mind* and, most recently, *The Trouble with Prosperity*. He currently writes a monthly column in *Forbes*.

Grant's Interest Rate Observer has a big-picture focus and a generally unique take on current events. Recent issues have featured detailed analyses of how banks are making fundamental mistakes that will lead to their undoing, how homeowners are overborrowing, how innovations like securitization and mortgage REITs are leading us to ruin, the relationship between stock prices and inflation, and the changing profile of central-bank balance sheets. The list goes on, seemingly forever, since Grant's ability to see patterns and analyze previously unexplored relationships in finance and business appears to be endless. And, icing on the cake, his newsletter is beautifully written, with a lot of bitingly funny cartoons.

J. Taylor's Gold & Technology Stocks
Editor: Jay Taylor
Since 1986
Frequency: Monthly
Trial subscription: $39 for three months
Annual rate: $123
P.O. Box 871
Woodside, NY 11377
Tel: (718) 457-1426
Web site: www.miningstocks.com
E-mail: info@miningstocks.com

A former Wall Street gold-mining analyst, Jay Taylor covers the whole spectrum of mining companies, with an emphasis on juniors. And he's been quite successful at finding emerging miners before they emerge: The newsletter's sample portfolio outperformed gold itself by 20 percentage points a year in 2002 and 2003.

Taylor offers a weekly telephone hot-line message that covers late-breaking news on the economy, gold, and his favorite stocks. But the main attraction is his in-depth but still quite readable reports, in which he explains in clear terms what an emerging miner is doing and whether it's likely to succeed. Here's a brief excerpt from a much longer report: "EmGold's major focus is a glorious old gold mine known as the Idaho-Maryland Mine, located in Grass Valley, California. This wasn't exactly a mom-and-pop operation, because it yielded 2,383,000 ounces of gold from 1862 through 1956. Emgold sees a little over 1 million ounces that it is planning to mine over a ten-year time frame, but as it is doing that, it is expected to develop gold reserves far below the 1,500 ft. maximum depth from which gold was produced in the past. In fact, part of the company's exploration plans in the near future call for a 5,000 ft. drill hole to test the depth extension of gold mineralization on this project."

International Harry Schultz Letter
Editor: Harry Schultz
Since 1964
Frequency: Monthly
Trial subscription: US$241for 8-month trial
Annual rate: US$327
P.O. Box 622
CH-1001 Lausanne, Switzerland
Tel: 011 506 271 2293 (from U.S. or Canada), 00 506 271 2293
(from any other country)
Web site: www.hsletter.com
E-mail: info@hsletter.com

No wallflower, Harry Schultz describes his letter as "the world's premier international investment, financial, economic, geopolitical, privacy, sociological and philosophical newsletter." But as the saying goes, it's not bragging if you can back it up. And Schultz's newsletter is in its fortieth successful year, with subscribers in eighty nations and a good overall record of both macro and stock-specific calls.

Based in Switzerland, Schultz draws on the analysis of correspondents in many countries and a first-rate in-house research staff. His newsletter casts such a wide net that to characterize it in a few sentences is impossible. Suffice it to say that it's a great overview of the world as seen through a sound-money lens, and a useful source of "how-to" information on diversifying out of dollars and into more promising currencies like the Swiss franc. One recent Schultz quote that we especially like: "A mega-derivative squeeze is coming . . . which will shred the present day gold cartel into confetti."

International Speculator
Editor: Doug Casey
Since 1979
Frequency: Monthly
Trial subscription: NA
Annual rate: $199
P.O. Box 84911
Phoenix, AZ 85071
Tel: (602) 252-4477; toll-free: (800) 528-0559
Web site: www.caseyresearch.com
E-mail: isp@publishers-mgmt.com

Doug Casey is the author of *Crisis Investing*, one of the best-selling financial books of the 1970s. Using what he calls a "rational speculation" strategy, he attempts to reduce excessive risk by identifying companies with the strongest management teams, shareholder-friendly capital structures, and promising properties.

These days he's focusing on well-managed junior exploration companies "that offer multiple opportunities to profit, for example when acquiring an attractive mineral concession, or reporting successful drilling results, or penning a joint development deal with a deep-pocketed large mining company." Any of those events, says Casey, has the potential to send a junior exploration company up by double or even triple digits, literally overnight. Another sector Casey was exploring in early 2004 was highly leveraged development companies that take advantage of low commodities prices to acquire properties that aren't economical at current prices but become so when commodities prices rise. The assumption is that their earnings—and market values—will soar in a commodities bull market.

Le Metropole Café
Proprietor: Bill Murphy
Since 1998
Frequency: Daily
Trial subscription: Two weeks free
Annual rate: $149
Web site: www.lemetropolecafe.com
E-mail: LePatron@LeMetropoleCafe.com

Le Metropole Café is a members-only "online community" modeled after early twentieth century French cafés like the Moulin Rouge. The idea is to create a space in which, as the home page puts it, "investors from all over the world can meet to discuss the vibrant economic and financial issues of the day." It succeeds admirably and is, in our opinion, the sound-money world's best online gathering place.

Led by Gold Antitrust Action Committee co-founder Bill Murphy, Le Metropole's "economic dream team" conducts an ongoing, high-level discussion of everything from global monetary policy to the ins and outs of metals trading. Not surprisingly, given Murphy's GATA connection, a central topic of debate is the war between the world's central banks and gold. If our chapter "The Great Central-Bank Short Squeeze" intrigued you, Le Metropole is the place to immerse yourself in the subject.

And because it's a Web site, it's interactive. That is, you can join the discussion by adding your own thoughts to the many "posting forums." In August 2004, there were active threads on dozens of topics, ranging from how to buy silver coins to the machinations of the Russian central bank. The result, as *Forbes* magazine recently noted, is a certain amount of hot air, but far more insight and excitement. Take the free two-week trial membership, and you'll more than likely be hooked for life.

Moneychanger
Editor: Franklin Sanders
Since 1980
Frequency: Monthly
Trial subscription: None, but full refund after three issues if not satisfied; prorated refund after that
Annual rate: $149
P.O. Box 178
Westpoint, TN 38486-0178
Tel: (888) 218-9226
Web site: www.the-moneychanger.com
E-mail: moneychanger@compuserve.com

Franklin Sanders uses his *Moneychanger* newsletter to offer a wide-ranging critique of the current system, along with advice on everything from Christianity to alternative health. But his main focus is precious-metals investing, and his newsletter features interviews with luminaries like Le Metropole Café founder Bill Murphy and silver guru Ted Butler, along with advice on buying gold coins, profiles of major and emerging miners, analyses of the flaws in today's banking system, and sophisticated options strategies. Sanders has also authored several books and pamphlets, including *The Next Great Depression* ($238), the *Gold, Silver and Platinum Report* ($38), and *Silver Bonanza,* coauthored with Jim Blanchard ($34).

Ormetal Report
Editor: Claude Cormier
Since 1996
Frequency: Semimonthly (24 per year)
Trial subscription: Free issue available online
Annual rate: US$149 (CAN$199). Or pay with GoldMoney for a 10-percent discount.
Ormetal Inc.
4004 Chemin du Lac Morgan
Rawdon, QC

Canada, J0K 1S0
Tel/Fax: (450) 834-8447
Web site: www.ormetal.com
E-mail: info@ormetal.com

Ormetal's Claude Cormier casts a wide net in his search for emerging mining stocks and has turned up winners from all over the world (recall the example of Francisco Gold on page 107). But his unique strength is his knowledge of the Canadian market. A must-read for advice on Canadian gold and silver juniors.

Resource Opportunities
Editor: Lawrence Roulston
Since 1997
Frequency: Approximately 20 issues per year
Trial subscription: Sample reports available online
Annual rate: $169 ($225 CDN)
625 Howe St.
Suite 1290
V6C 2T6, Vancouver, BC
Canada
Tel: (604) 697-0026; toll-free: (877) 773-7677
Web site: www.resourceopportunities.com
E-mail:info@resourceopportunities.com

Lawrence Roulston is a trained geologist with more than twenty years of firsthand experience in the resource industry, including several years as the president of a mining-exploration company. His newsletter is well written and easily accessible, with jargon-free prose and an insider's perspective. He explores issues like the rise of China and the debasement of the dollar with clarity, but in enough depth to allow readers to understand the process. He also offers detailed profiles of what he considers the most interesting, least risky resource plays. "*Resource Opportunities* stays away from the riskiest of the juniors, those exploration companies that are simply rolling the dice on a drill play," says Roulston. "Instead, the newsletter focuses on companies that have already outlined a deposit, but where more work is required to prove up a reserve."

Such miners "are typically valued at steep discounts compared to the larger producers. In fact, some of those small companies trade at values that equate to only a few dollars an ounce for gold in the ground. That compares to a typical valuation in excess of $100 an ounce for the major producers. [This] smaller company approach provides enormous leverage to the gold market. Your investment gives you the benefit of owning many more ounces than if you invested in a major producer."

The Silver Investor Newsletter
Editor: David Morgan
Frequency: Monthly
Trial subscription: $60 for 3 months
Annual rate: $149 hard copy in U.S., $169 international, $99 e-mail
Stone Investment Group
21307 Buckeye Lake Lane
Colbert, WA 99005
Tel (toll-free): (877) 610-9962
Web site: www.silver-investor.com
E-mail: silverguru22@hotmail.com

Silver Investor is the only newsletter listed here that focuses primarily on silver. Editor David Morgan's emphasis is on silver-mining stocks, though he spends a fair amount of time on the macro environment. Past issues include analyses of silver stockpiles (they're shrinking), the manipulation of the silver market by players trying to keep it cheap (why they'll fail), the impact of digital photography on silver demand (minimal), and silver's role in solving the energy crisis (pivotal).

The heart of *Silver Investor* is Morgan's "Model Portfolio," which is divided into two sections: cash-rich mining companies and "silver speculations." The list is relatively short, reflecting the currently small number of active silver plays.

WEB SITES
(in alphabetical order)

www.321gold.com

www.a1-guide-to-gold-investments.com

www.capitalupdates.com

www.depression2.tv

www.fame.org

www.financialsense.com

www.gata.org

www.goldcolony.com

www.gold-eagle.com

www.goldenbar.com

www.goldensextant.com

www.goldismoney.infoindex.html

www.goldmoney.com

www.goldseek.com

www.howestreet.com

www.investmentrarities.com

www.jsmineset.com

www.kitco.com

www.mineralstox.com

www.minesite.com

www.mineweb.com

www.mininglife.com

www.mises.org

www.moneyfiles.org

mwhodges.home.att.net

www.sharelynx.com

www.silverseek.com

www.theaureport.com

www.thebulliondesk.com

TOMORROW'S GOLD STANDARD

Gold still represents the ultimate form of payment in the world.

—ALAN GREENSPAN,
Testimony before the U.S. House Banking Committee, 1999

In this book, we've addressed two questions of immediate importance: Why is the dollar going to collapse, and how can gold both protect you and enable you to profit from the coming monetary crisis? We've purposely avoided speculating about what comes after, both because it's uncertain and because the subject deserves a book of its own, which we hope to write once those events begin to unfold.

But it's hard not to wonder how the world will look after so much of today's conventional wisdom has been tossed aside. And it's hard not to worry. Historically, currency collapses have led to awful changes in political and economic systems (think Rome being sacked by the Visigoths or the rise of Napoleon in France). And since the mess now in the works is bigger in both size and scope than anything that's come before, the suffering could be correspondingly worse.

So, is the industrialized world headed the way of Imperial Rome, or can humanity find a way to make lemonade from this decade's financial lemons? When the dollar implodes, and then the yen and euro, and the whole concept of fiat currency is thrown into disrepute, what money will step in to fill the void? Will governments be able to resurrect their failed currencies in a new monetary system, or will we return to the gold standard, assuming it's feasible?

Obviously, at this point no one knows the answers to these questions. But we're willing to go on record with some thoughts on what *should* happen. We support a return to an objective standard of value independent of government interference as the only logical way for the coming mess to be resolved. This is also a moral imperative, because sound money is, after all, an ethical as well as economic issue. Our currency is the promise we make to ourselves, our children, and our trading partners that our word is and will be good, that the value we receive today will be repaid with equal value in the future. And in all of human history, only gold has been able to fulfill this promise.

Now, you could argue that in a sense we never really left the gold standard. Though nations long ago broke the contract that linked their currencies to gold, gold has remained the world's numeraire, the standard against which other things are measured. Recall the chart on page 42 depicting the gold price of oil, and it becomes clear that gold has continued to function in this way, without the sanction or cooperation—and sometimes with the enmity—of the world's central banks. Though you can't redeem dollars for gold at the U.S. Treasury, you can trade dollars for gold on global exchanges, twenty-four hours a day. And the behavior of the world's central banks implies that the gold exchange rate remains a key measure of a currency's success.

As the dollar collapse metastasizes into a global currency implosion, the world will come to yet another crossroad. In one direction will lie even greater centralization of political and economic power (let's call this Scenario One), in which the result, as it was in the 1930s, is collective action in the form of bigger, more authoritarian government. If we start down this road, with government spending already accounting for half of many national economies, the result will be something akin to Eastern

Europe in the 1980s: centrally planned systems in which bureaucrats decide nearly everything. Money, in this ugly but all too plausible world, will be whatever the dictator *du jour* says it is. And gold will be driven underground and/or confiscated as it was in the 1930s.

We won't delve further into this scenario. It's too familiar, since variations of it have existed—and still do, for that matter—in countries all over the world. If it comes to pass, all bets are off. We simply have no advice to offer, other than to fight the process to the best of your ability and/or keep your head down.

But what if, this time, the disaster awakens people to the risks inherent in money substitutes and causes them to demand an alternative? We won't have to look far for a blueprint. A simple return to the Constitution's original intent would suffice. In practical terms, that means restricting the role of government to a few essential functions. And it means making currency independent of the whims of politicians and their constituents. How? Again, we don't have to look far. When the debate turns to creating a sound monetary system, the loudest, most convincing voices will be those calling for a return to gold, which is again one of the great legacies of the framers. Recall from Chapter 8 that they made gold and silver this country's money, and enshrined it (or at least tried to enshrine it) for future generations in Article I of the Constitution.

So let's sketch out two hopeful timelines, in which, confronted with a global currency collapse, we draw the proper conclusions and make the right choices:

SCENARIO TWO:
THE WORLD COMES TO ITS SENSES

2005: The dollar is in full retreat on foreign exchange markets, and panic is building on both Wall Street and Main Street. Dollar-denominated bonds plunge in value, which is another way of saying that long-term interest rates soar. Spiking mortgage rates and restrictions on access to new lending burst the housing bubble in overheated markets like California and New York. Home prices drop by 50 percent or more in the space of a few months, and the leaders of the structured finance sector, mortgage giants Fannie Mae and Freddie Mac and derivatives players like JP Morgan Chase, are revealed as the time bombs they are. Their stocks, and most others associated with the U.S. credit bubble, begin to slide. The euro and yen soar against the dollar, while gold blows through $1,000 ($32.15/gg) without a backward glance.

2006: European and Asian leaders, seeing their vital export sectors lose ground because of their soaring currencies, fight back by cutting interest rates and intervening in foreign exchange markets. Competitive devaluations reminiscent of the 1930s become the new global economic policy. The Dollar Disease spreads to the euro and yen, as those once-powerful currencies begin to fall, not against the dollar, which is still reeling, but against gold, oil, and other tangible assets. The prices of many commodities soar, as consumers the world over convert their paper currencies and other financial assets into real goods and services as quickly as possible at whatever price. The flight from currency is in full swing.

A major U.S. financial institution fails spectacularly, and access to capital dries up for the rest. No one wants to invest in, or lend to, such companies, and speculation is rampant about which will be next to die. Major governments, meanwhile, begin to flirt with capital controls, price controls, and other desperate measures. Voices on the right call for strengthened national-security laws, while those on the left demand a government bailout of homeowners and tottering banks, along with jobs programs to keep the economy moving. All sides of the political spectrum demand "strong leadership." Certain civil and economic liberties are "temporarily" suspended. Gold breaks $2,000 ($64.31/gg).

2007: While the world's governments panic, its people, aided by the Internet and other modern media, begin educating themselves and debating the causes and cures of their dilemma. As in the nineteenth century, when discussions of monetary policy were common, highly public, and followed by the masses, crucial issues like the true nature of money and the inability of governments to manage their national currencies become front-page news. And gradually, an understanding begins to form that these problems are neither acts of God nor the result of too much freedom or too small and lenient a government. Instead, they're the result of our unwillingness, at every level of society, to live within our means.

The next few months are remarkable: an electronic-age version of the Constitutional Convention, in which the U.S. returns to its philosophical roots and examines the source material of its culture. And the debate turns away from how to structure a dictatorship to see us through, and toward how to re-create the original conception of liberal democracy. The realization spreads that money substitutes have had their day in the sun, and all eyes turn to gold, the one form of money that has held its value while paper currencies have been converted to so much confetti.

One of the major impediments to a return to gold in 2003 was the fact that, at $400 an ounce ($12.86/gg), there was only about $2 trillion of it available, far too little to supply a $32 trillion global economy with money. By 2007, that's no longer a problem. Gold's exchange rate has soared to around $5,000 ($160.77/gg), making the available supply worth about $25 trillion, while its velocity—the frequency at which each ounce changes hands in the economy—has been increased by the latest electronic transactions technologies. Put another way, the dollar has been devalued to the point where gold's exchange rate is over ten times as high, making the supply of gold quite adequate for the global economy, and rather than idling away in vaults, gold is circulating as the world's only non-national currency.

2008: A new generation of politicians, whether through real conviction or opportunism, seizes the moment and demands a return to sound money and fiscal sanity. A majority of citizens now understand that these goals can be achieved only by (1) choosing as money something that can't be debased and (2) limiting the ability of governments and citizens to mortgage their futures by borrowing too much in the here and now. Days after her inauguration, the first "post-dollar" president proposes legislation limiting federal transfer programs and scaling back government spending in nearly every other sphere. She announces that henceforth the New Gold Dollar will be permanently convertible into gold, digital or physical, at a rate based on current market reality.

And to keep future generations from forgetting the lessons of the twentieth century, a Constitutional Convention is called, to put into writing what the Framers intuitively understood: that only one thing—gold—will serve as money, and that all other things will be valued and priced in relation to it.

SCENARIO THREE:
THE MARKETS CHOOSE GOLD

2006: As the dollar's collapse turns into a generalized global flight from fiat currencies, one functioning currency holds its own: digital gold. Recall from Chapter 19 that several such currencies were operating in 2003, and that they offer the advantages of gold money with none of the disadvantages. Seeing holders of digital gold prospering while holders of dollars and euros are ruined, investors convert increasing amounts of capital to these new currencies, creating a virtuous cycle in which rising demand for digital gold sends its exchange rate higher, making it even more attractive and drawing in more capital. Smaller countries begin adopting digital gold as their official currency, and pressure begins to mount on large countries to follow suit.

2007: Central bankers, horrified at the collapse of both their fiat currencies and the intellectual rationale for their careers, resist with all the power at their disposal. But since their powers rest on their ability to manipulate currencies that are rapidly becoming worthless, they gradually relent or are replaced by younger colleagues with less philosophical baggage. And the world, despite the best efforts of its monetary authorities, returns to gold. The Age of Paper ends with a whimper rather than a bang, and humanity's last currency crisis is now history.

Which of these three futures will we choose? History, unfortunately, favors dictatorship. But history isn't destiny. Past societies lacked today's global mass media and sophisticated, adaptable capital markets. So the other, more hopeful scenarios are at least feasible. In any event, this discussion is one for another day. Right now, we have yet another currency collapse to deal with.

INDEX